# Your Retirement Salary

Every owner of a physical copy of this edition of

# Your Retirement Salary

can download the eBook for free direct from us at Harriman House, in a DRM-free format that can be read on any eReader, tablet or smartphone.

Simply head to:

## ebooks.harriman-house.com/ retirementsalary

to get your copy now.

# Your Retirement Salary

How to use your lifetime of pension savings to pay yourself an income in retirement

Richard Dyson
and Richard Evans

Hh

Hh Harriman House

HARRIMAN HOUSE LTD
18 College Street
Petersfield
Hampshire
GU31 4AD
GREAT BRITAIN

Tel: +44 (0)1730 233870
Email: enquiries@harriman-house.com
Website: www.harriman-house.com

First published in Great Britain in 2019
Copyright © Richard Dyson and Richard Evans

The right of Richard Dyson and Richard Evans to be identified as the authors has
been asserted in accordance with the Copyright, Design and Patents Act 1988.

Paperback ISBN: 978-0-85719-567-8
eBook ISBN: 978-0-85719-568-5

British Library Cataloguing in Publication Data
A CIP catalogue record for this book can be obtained from the British Library.

# About the authors

## Richard Dyson

Richard Dyson is a prize-winning financial journalist with a 20-year career writing for many of Britain's leading media groups and specialist investor titles, including the *Express*, *Mail on Sunday*, *Investors Chronicle*, and the *Daily Telegraph* and *Sunday Telegraph*.

He was previously Head of Personal Finance at the Telegraph Media Group, where he oversaw all the personal finance and investment writing across the Telegraph titles and websites.

He has won numerous awards for financial writing including, in 2016, being named the Personal Finance Society's Journalist of the Year.

He conceived the *Telegraph's* widely followed Questor Income Portfolio, a publicly tracked portfolio of 25 stocks and bonds aimed squarely at retired investors who seek income.

Launched at a time when the Bank of England's Base Rate was just 0.25%, the portfolio has succeeded in generating its target 5% income.

## Richard Evans

Richard Evans is one of Britain's leading investment commentators and an expert on the enormous range of funds – such as unit trusts and investment trusts – available to individual savers.

His knowledge has been largely amassed through one-on-one interviews with fund managers and other professional investors over the course of many years.

With a particular interest in sustainable income investing, Richard Evans invented the "1% rule" – fully explained in this book – which enables non-specialist savers to ensure they do not deplete their investments too quickly.

Richard Evans currently edits the *Daily Telegraph's* Questor share-tipping column. He was previously Personal Finance Editor of the *Daily Telegraph*.

# Contents

# Preface

Everyone needs income in retirement.

You may be an experienced investor who has overseen your pension money for some years. Or you may be approaching retirement knowing next to nothing about pensions and the stock market.

Either way, if you are in your 50s or older and have pension savings of as much as £1m or as little as £30,000, this book can help you. Its aim is to equip you with everything you need to turn years of pension savings into income that will last through your retirement.

This book is not about saving towards your future retirement: it's about what to do with the money you've already saved up as you near retirement and then during your retirement.

It's been written in response to the new pension rules introduced in April 2015. In essence, these rules give you the freedom to use your pension cash as you wish, once you're over 55. These dramatic rule changes could be hugely advantageous to you, or they could result in you making disastrous slip-ups, such as paying thousands of pounds in unnecessary tax, or running out of money.

As you read, you will learn:

- Enough about the new pension regime to be confident overseeing your own money.

- How to build and maintain a portfolio of investments to provide an income for life.

- How to select the companies where you will hold your pension investments – and the investments themselves – in a way that will minimise your costs.

- How to pay less tax.

- When you should seek professional advice and how much to pay for it.

This book makes pensions simple. We avoid unnecessary jargon, and carefully explain the terms we do use. And we don't include anything that's not essential and useful.

## How this book is structured

The book is divided into three parts. The first covers the basic knowledge of pensions that you are likely to require and the preparations that you'll need to make before you can put your pension assets to use in generating income. The second describes what is involved in actually setting up and running your income-producing portfolios, including the hugely important task of ensuring that your income is sustainable. The final part covers various supplementary but vital topics: minimising the amount of tax you pay, the role of the state pension, topping up your pension if necessary by releasing money from your home, and how and when to seek professional financial advice.

## A note on investing and portfolios

The process described in this book will require you to gradually work up to a point where you are comfortable investing in company shares and bonds, via funds managed by professional investors, to build your own income portfolio.

This might be new ground for you – perhaps you have never invested in shares and bonds before, and perhaps you are not really sure what a fund is and how it works. Maybe the very word *investing* sounds complicated and something better left to the professionals. Do not be daunted.

There is nothing arcane or unusual in these investments – they are the same assets that pension funds have invested in for decades on behalf of their clients. Yes, there are risks involved, but they can be carefully managed.

As we will see throughout the course of this book, it is now becoming increasingly necessary for retirees to take matters into their own hands and look after their own pension savings during their retirement. It is also easier than ever before for you to do this.

# Introduction

Every year the Money Desk at the *Daily Telegraph* receives thousands of emails and letters. They relate to everything from disastrous holidays, to flooded homes, to pet insurers that wouldn't pay for the family dog's hypnotherapy.

But increasingly they're about pensions.

Pensions are becoming more of a worry for everyone, not just the elderly and the hard-up. Pensions are in the news week in, week out. They are near the top of the political agenda for every party, whatever its leanings. Pensions pose serious problems for business and indeed for society as a whole.

In the end, though, making the most of your pension is down to you. Almost all of the pension-related queries sent to the *Telegraph* are from individuals grappling to understand their own pension arrangements better.

Many of the questions cover similar ground. The following, for example, were received within a day or two as this book was being written. They are representative of hundreds more.

- "I have saved £400 per month into a pension for 17 years but now aged 55 I have no idea where it is. How can I find out?"

- "I have six pensions, but I've been told they will pay me only £740 per year in total. Can this be right?"

- "I have reached pension age but am still working. Can I save more?"

- "I'm 60 and I have saved £75,000 into a pension. What shall I do with it?"

- "I've been told that obtaining a return on my pension investments of 4% is about all I can safely hope for. Is that true?"

Questions such as these are becoming more frequent. In the past, employers tended to handle pension affairs for their staff and made difficult decisions on their behalf.

But, as we explain, that's now changing. Understanding your pension, and getting the most out of it, are now your responsibility. And it's the realisation of that fact that is causing a sudden spike in the number of calls for help.

This book answers all the above questions and, more than that, it provides a complete, structured guide to organising your pension money and making it pay an income for life.

# Prologue: How much income can I expect from my pension savings – and will it be enough?

The first thing you want to know if you have a sum of money set aside for retirement is, how much income will it produce?

In this book we outline an approach to investing that money so that it will produce an income of between 3% and 5% a year.

In other words, anyone with £100,000 saved up can expect an income of £3,000–£5,000 a year, while those who have accumulated £300,000 will get between £9,000 and £15,000 a year.

We aim to increase these amounts roughly in line with inflation every year.

Why is there a range of numbers? We have aimed to cater to a broad audience with differing needs. Some will want to "sweat their assets" and receive the highest possible income for every £1 they have saved. Others will have one eye on the amount they can leave to their children and will therefore want to take less out of their savings pot for themselves.

We think 5% is the most that can safely be taken in income from a pot of savings every year, while 3% is more conservative and should allow plenty to be left for the next generation.

Later in this book we suggest two portfolios of investments aimed at producing those two incomes, 3% and 5%, along with a third portfolio that aims for 4% and is intended for those whose needs fall somewhere between the other two groups

Now we have said that 5% is the maximum that we think you can safely take as income from your pension savings each year, the question "will it be enough?" arises.

Let's say you have £200,000 in your pension. Taking the maximum of 5% will give you £10,000 a year. Assuming that you qualify for the full state pension of about £8,000, you can expect £18,000 a year in total.

If you are in any doubt about whether you will be able to live the life you want on that money, you'll need to draw up a budget of all your likely annual expenditure in retirement, to arrive at a total (we describe how to do this in Chapter Four).

Should your expected income fall short of your likely expenditure, your choices are to live more frugally in retirement, save more into your pension while you are still working, or carry on working for longer. We discuss working beyond the normal retirement age in Chapter Nine.

# Before we start, a word of warning...

Everything in this book is based on the idea that you will invest your money in assets such as shares in order to generate income. *All investing involves risk.* Neither the authors nor anyone else can offer a way to invest that provides the incomes we aim to achieve without taking risk.

We believe that the approach we adopt here keeps the risk as small as possible relative to the outcomes we are aiming for. But if you could not tolerate, for example, a fall in the value of your savings or a fall in income as a result of declines in investments, you should not proceed with the course of action described in the book and should instead put your pension savings into guaranteed assets such as cash and annuities.

The suggestions in this book are not intended to constitute personal financial advice. The circumstances of each person are different and the general framework we outline will need to be adapted to your own financial position and that of your family, and to your goals and risk tolerance. If in doubt seek personalised advice from a financial adviser regulated by the Financial Conduct Authority.

# Part One

## Getting Prepared

This part covers the first steps that you need to take before you can begin to invest your pension money to generate income. This includes understanding the basics of Britain's pension system and getting all your various pots of money together in one place.

# Chapter One
# Britain's Pension Earthquake

**"Why do I need to think about my pension?"**

IN THIS CHAPTER, WE DESCRIBE what a pension is. Then we explain how the pensions landscape has changed dramatically in recent years, with millions of people now able to manage their own pension savings to generate a retirement income.

We explain the conditions that led to the demise of Britain's generous employer-funded pensions and how these same conditions affect a new generation of people managing their own pensions. The chapter ends with definitions of ten pieces of pensions jargon you will see mentioned again and again.

It is important that you understand this background because problems that would previously have been resolved by employers are now going to become problems that individuals need to resolve on their own. This chapter explains how and why this has come about.

However, we appreciate that some will already be aware of this background and will want to get straight down to the job. If this is you, then you can safely skip this chapter and turn to Chapter Two.

## What is a pension?

Simple: a pension is the money you live on when you've retired.

Beyond that, there are some other definitions. Sometimes the word pension is used to mean a regular income, similar to a weekly or monthly wage; the state pension, for example. When someone is already retired, they are likely to be describing a regular income when they use the word pension. "I can just manage on a pension of £250 per week," someone might say.

But at other times a pension describes a sum of money, or an investment portfolio that is earmarked for retirement. This is what people mean when they use the term *pension pot*.

The pot is what's been accumulated over the decades of a working life, made up of your own savings out of your income, plus tax breaks from the government and probably some contributions from your employer. This pot is *not* an income in itself; it's a pool of money that you have saved while you were working and that will need, somehow, to be turned into an income at the point of your retirement from work.

Another use of the word pension is in referring to pension income entitlements, or benefits that you have built up through work that won't be paid until you reach a set retirement age. These guaranteed entitlements usually apply only to older, and now less common, *final salary* work pensions. There is more about this type of pension below in this chapter and also in Chapter Two.

## How pensions used to be

Older generations will recognise the concept of giving a gold watch to long-serving staffers on the day of their retirement. Younger generations will never have heard of such a thing.

The gold watch was a tradition. If someone retired after, say, 25 or 30 years' work with the same firm, the watch would be presented to the retiree by way of thanks. "You have given the company years of your life, now your time will be your own."

The pension of the past was very much tied up with this paternalistic style of employment. If you worked for a big firm in the sixties, seventies or eighties, the chances are you belonged to the company's pension scheme. And by today's standards, the pension would probably be extremely generous. What's more, it was the firm's responsibility to pay you the promised income for life when you retired.

Individual employees faced no difficult decisions about where, when or how to invest money. It was all taken care of on their behalf. Come the end of your career, you collected the watch, went home, and what had been your earned wage in one month became your pension payment the next month. This was called a *defined benefit* company pension, as the pension you received on retirement was defined by the company. These are also known as final salary pensions.

For example, say you worked for 25 years with the same company and at retirement you were earning £55,000. Your pension would be linked to both your final salary and your length of service. A typical formula might grant one fortieth of final salary towards your pension for every year served. In that case your pension in this example would be £34,375 (25 years x 1/40 x £55,000).

Not everyone benefited to the same degree. But for millions this was the process by which comfortable retirement incomes were built. Many older people today – those in their 70s and 80s – are still benefiting from these generous, guaranteed arrangements, and as they look at how their children are faring in relation to pension saving they are realising how lucky they were.

When it is said that "the British pension system is the envy of the world", it is generally this era of pension provision that's being referred to. And sadly that era is no more.

## Why the good days came to an end – and why it matters

*What killed off the generous work pensions of yesteryear?*

This may sound like an academic question, but the answers have direct relevance to those who will need to look after their own pension income today.

You can boil it down to just two factors.

*The first is that people's lifespans have mushroomed.*

While today we generally expect our parents and grandparents to live into their 80s and 90s, reaching such ages is a surprisingly recent phenomenon. On average, anyone born before 1940 did not make it to 70.

Today, a man who has reached the age of 65 is expected to live another 19 years. A woman of 65 today will live another 21 years. These are averages, based on statistics crunched by the government and other institutions. In reality, of course, your own longevity is unlikely to exactly match the average. But what these average figures show is a dramatic, and largely unexpected, lengthening in lifespans. That has generally meant longer retirements – which cost more.

---

In what year will you die? Find the latest average life expectancy for your age and sex in the table on page 55 in Chapter Three.

---

When companies promised to pay staff a pension for life after they retired, say, at age 62, those companies may not have imagined that they might still be paying that pension 30 or even 40 years later.

Because companies are under strict obligations to regularly recalculate the likely cost of pension promises, based on up-to-date longevity statistics, we are now very familiar with gloomy news regarding pensions and big business. Business deals have fallen through because past pension promises have been deemed to be unaffordable. Some businesses have failed entirely because of such promises and the government has had to step in with a range of rescue arrangements.

---

"£1 trillion – The size of the total funding 'black hole' in UK final salary pension schemes" [*Telegraph*, 23 August 2016]

"Tesco setback as pension black hole balloons to £5bn" [*Telegraph*, 24 September 2016]

"Vauxhall pension black hole could be stumbling block for GM sale to Peugeot" [*Telegraph*, 20 February 2017]

"FTSE 100 heavyweights jolted by £95bn surge in pension liabilities" [*Telegraph*, 29 August 2017]

"BT brokers deal to shut final salary pension" [*Telegraph*, 20 March 2018]

---

*The second factor is falling investment returns.*

The assumptions about returns on investments change over the years. People whose main working and investing lives were in the 1970s, 1980s and 1990s would have a very different idea of normal rates of return from investments from, say, someone in their mid-30s today, whose only experience of saving and investing has been in the past decade.

Experience of the past forms our expectations of the future. And, as the statistics in Table 1.1 show, investment returns in the past were very different – and much higher. The shares column shows that while the early 1970s were difficult, the stock market did very well in general throughout most of the second half of the 20th century. Annual returns averaging 9% for the period 1986 to 1996 are, for example, far higher than the returns we have become used to in recent decades.

The cash column shows the real return from cash deposits for the periods stated, which means the interest earned by cash after inflation is taken into account. These return figures for cash show a similar decline to that seen for shares: the negative figure for the period

2006–2016 shows that cash deposits lost value in this period. Overall what is clear is that cash currently produces very low returns.

**Table 1.1: Average returns per year, after inflation: the 80s and 90s saw better investment returns**

| Decade | Shares | Cash |
|--------|--------|------|
| 1956–1966 | 7.8% | 1.8% |
| 1966–1976 | −0.3% | −2% |
| 1976–1986 | 14.6% | 2.6% |
| 1986–1996 | 9% | 4.9% |
| 1996–2006 | 4.9% | 2.6% |
| 2006–2016 | 2.5% | −1.3% |

Source: Barclays Equity Gilt Study 2017.

As companies were crippled with rising pension costs associated with their former employees living longer, they were also hit with lower returns on the investments they made to meet those costs. It was a fatal double whammy.

While companies are bound by law to deliver pension promises made in the past, they do not have to offer similarly generous pensions to current workers and future retirees. And so they don't.

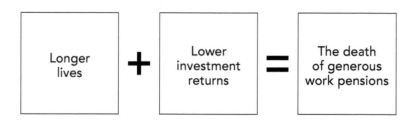

In the past, the thorny issues of how long you might live, and how much it would cost to provide income for that indefinite period, was your employer's problem. They paid your pension, so they had to find the money, somehow.

But, as explained below in relation to the rise of the *pension pot*, now those problems have become yours. You don't know how long you are going to live. You don't know how many years of income you are going to need. And you are going to have to make your own investment choices and other financial decisions about how best to make your retirement money last.

It's not the purpose of this book to explain why investment returns have fallen in recent decades. But, as you will see in Chapters Four and Five, you need to choose your investments now on the basis that returns may continue to be low for some time to come.

Longer lives and lower returns – the very things that put an end to the great company pensions of yesteryear – will also be the two big factors that shape the decisions people take with their retirement money in the years and decades to come.

## The rise and rise of the pension pot

The death of the old-style, generous company pensions where your employer paid you a retirement income for life has given rise instead to the *pension pot* method of retirement saving.

Apart from teachers, NHS employees and others in certain civil service roles, virtually no one who is working today has any other type of pension arrangement. For most people, it's all about building a pension pot.

The technical term for the pension pot type of retirement funding is *defined contribution*. It's something of a laboured term, typical of actuaries and insurance companies. It means your company pays a set amount towards your eventual pension each month: a defined contribution. For example, each month at the same time as paying your salary, your employer automatically puts a part of your salary – say 2% – into a pension. Your employer also makes its own additional contribution to the pension – which may be the same percentage as that taken from your salary, or it may be more or less than that percentage. It is these percentages that are the defined contribution.

What happens to the pension contributions after that is down to where the money is invested by the pension provider, how those investments perform and a good dollop of luck. When you come to retire, the total amount of money in the pot is your pension. At that point of retirement, the owner of the pension pot – that is you, the retiree – has a big decision to make about what to do with the money.

Unlike with the old schemes, which as we saw were known as *defined benefit*, with the pension pot arrangement your company makes no promises about what income you will receive in your retirement; only the *contribution* made to the pension pot is defined. That distinction is crucial. This is how the burden for providing income during retirement has shifted from the employer to the employee; from business to the individual.

If you have made monthly pension contributions from your salary with your current employer or past employers – which will have been shown on your payslip – then you will have one or more of these defined contribution pension pots. We describe how to get them organised in Chapter Two.

The shift towards the pension pot style of saving has been under way for decades. But developments in 2015 suddenly made it a great deal more significant.

## The pensions revolution of 2015

History has still to assess the legacy of George Osborne, the chancellor under David Cameron during the latter's term as prime minister. What is beyond doubt is that Osborne changed the landscape of personal finance more than any of his predecessors in living memory. He did this by tearing up the pension rule book.

His real objective? No one knows. Was it a political belief in freedom of choice for individuals, as Osborne said; or was it about saving money for the government at a time when the national debt was spiralling out of control?

---

"These freedoms are based on the simple idea that people know better how to spend their own money than governments do."

*George Osborne*

---

In a nutshell, under Mr Osborne's reforms, savers would be able to access their pension savings once they reached the age of 55. They could take as little or as much of the money as they wanted and spend it on whatever they liked. Gone were the restrictions that had previously required the money to be used to provide an income in retirement. As Mr Osborne said so emphatically: "No one will have to buy an annuity."

As far as you are concerned, in a practical sense these reforms mean that it has become your task to turn your pension cash into an income you can live on throughout retirement.

This was viewed as a positive step in most quarters. In the opinion of *Daily Telegraph* readers, it was warmly welcomed and seen, if anything, as long overdue.

Annuities had by then become the enemy of many pension savers. For those who don't know or who need reminding, an annuity is a form of insurance policy. You buy the policy with a cash lump sum at the point of your retirement. In return, the insurer pays you an income for life.

The insurance element is in the fact that no one knows how long you will live. If you live for a very long time you are protected: the income will keep on coming, and it will be the insurer's loss. If on the other hand you die shortly after buying the annuity, you lose out and the insurer benefits from a windfall.

Before George Osborne, pension rules had made it more or less impossible to avoid using some or all of your pension pot to buy an annuity. But falling annuity rates – the amount of income insurers offered in return for a lump sum paid by someone of a certain age – had made them deeply unpopular. By the time that Mr Osborne's pension freedoms were announced, annuity rates had roughly halved in just ten years.

In other words, you needed twice as much capital to buy the same retirement income.

---

## The rocketing cost of an annuity

You're 65 years old. You want to buy an inflation-linked income for life (annuity) starting at £35,000 per year.

Cost of this annuity in 2006: £761,000

Cost of the same annuity in 2019: £1.1m

Or, looking at this the other way around: You're 65 years old. You want to buy an inflation-linked income for life (annuity) with your pension pot of £761,000.

Annual income from annuity in 2006: £35,000

Annual income from annuity in 2019: £24,500

---

Annuity rates express as a percentage the income you buy with your lump sum. So a 5% annuity rate would mean an annual income of £5,000 for every £100,000 spent. Chart 1.1 shows how annuity rates have fallen.

**Chart 1.1: Falling annuity rates**

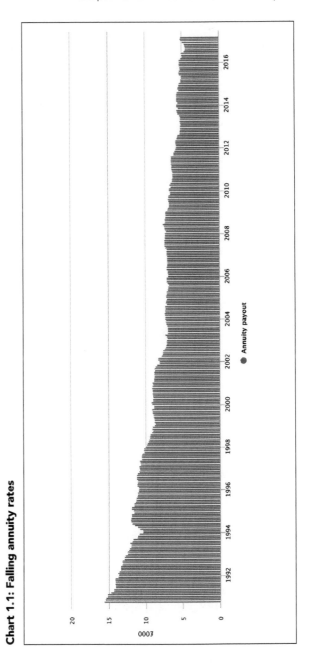

It's fair to say that annuity returns have become pretty poor. The fact that the pre-2015 pension rules virtually required you to buy an annuity was viewed as deeply unfair. Mr Osborne provided the key to freedom.

## Falling annuity rates

You might be reading this and wondering just why annuity rates have fallen so much and so consistently over the years. This is a technical subject and largely beyond the scope of this book, but very broadly the causes of this are the same two causes cited above for the end of defined benefit pensions: increasing life expectancies and falling investment returns.

# The Lamborghini moment

George Osborne's sudden liberalisation of the pension rules took politicians on all sides by surprise.

Not everyone welcomed the move. There were some who argued that the whole purpose of a pension system was to encourage individuals, through the provision of generous tax breaks, to build up an income that would last them through the final years of their lives. The state would thus be spared the cost of supporting them in old age. This fundamental contract or purpose was being broken by Mr Osborne, it was argued, if now savers could do whatever they wished with the cash from age 55.

In the political debates and interviews that followed the announcement of the reforms, the pensions minister at the time, Steve Webb, raised the idea of "taking all your pension and spending it on a Lamborghini". The concept stuck and, perversely, this Italian sports car marque has now become permanently associated with the somewhat less glamorous subject of pensions.

But the Lamborghini reference was effective: it underlined the sudden breadth of choice available to savers in their 50s and beyond. If they wanted to withdraw their entire pension savings as cash aged 55 and buy a sports car, they could do that. With that choice comes huge potential advantages – as well as dangers. We'll cover some of these opportunities and risks in the following chapters.

* * *

We've looked at what a pension is and we've seen how, in a few crucial steps, the problem of providing it has moved from employers to the individual.

In Chapter Two we look at how to take control of the pension investments and entitlements you already have. But before that, there are a few pension terms that everyone needs to be aware of.

## Ten pension terms you need to know in order to survive retirement

There's a glossary at the back of this book as well as an index. So hopefully you're not going to come across anything in the text that's going to stump you. In addition to that, in order to get the most out of the chapters that follow, there is a handful of basic terms that you cannot survive without.

These terms will appear on your work pension statements. They'll appear on your state pension statements. And they'll probably crop up in any documents or advice you are ever given by a financial adviser, if and when you turn to one for help (see Chapter Eleven).

### 1. Defined benefit

This describes the old-style, generous form of company pension that promised an income in retirement linked to your wage when you worked. Hence these were also called final salary pensions.

With these pensions the retirement income (benefit) was guaranteed (defined).

## 2. Defined contribution

This is the newer, pension pot style of company pension. Here your company isn't promising you a set level of income or defined benefit. Instead, it's just promising to pay a set amount (a defined contribution) into your pension pot. How much that turns into is then down to investment returns, time and luck. Personal pensions are also of the defined contribution type.

## 3. Pension pot

This is the sum total of money at your disposal in retirement, held within one or more pension accounts. It could be a company pension (of the defined contribution sort, above) or a personal pension – or you may have several of either or both. It's not an income in itself.

## 4. Contracted out

Britain's state pension system has undergone countless changes. Under previous systems, if you were in a company pension you could contract out of the secondary state pension, sometimes called SERPS (State Earnings Related Pension Scheme). This was a top-up state pension to boost your basic state pension.

If you contracted out, your company benefited through a reduction in National Insurance contributions. And an amount equivalent to the top-up would have been paid into another pension account. You may come across references to this as you bring your pension pots together.

SERPS ran from 6 April 1978 to 5 April 2002, at which point it was replaced by the State Second Pension. The State Second Pension was then replaced by the new – and existing – "flat rate" or "single tier" state pension arrangement on 6 April 2016.

## 5. Annuity

This is a policy provided by an insurer that converts a cash sum into an income for life. How much income you get depends on your age and health.

Annuities come with different provisions. Some offer income that rises each year to accommodate increases in the cost of living. These are known as inflation-linked annuities and they are more expensive. You can also choose for the payment to continue to a spouse after your death. This provision also costs more.

## 6. Tax relief

This is the government's carrot to get people to save into a pension. Within limits, what you pay into a pension will benefit from tax given back to you at the highest rate of income tax you pay. So a 20% taxpayer can contribute £80 towards a pension and receive £20 in tax relief, making the total amount added to the pension £100. A 40% taxpayer contributes just £60, then receives £40 in tax rebates for a £100 total contribution.

## 7. Tax-free lump sum

At age 55 with personal pensions, and at later ages with company pensions, up to 25% of your pension savings can be taken as a tax-free lump sum.

The rest of your pension money – the other 75% – becomes liable to tax when withdrawn.

## 8. Platform

This word is used to describe stockbrokers, ISA providers, fund shops or fund supermarkets – basically any firm that offers pension accounts where you are likely to be overseeing your own investments.

## 9. State pension age

This is the age at which you can claim your state pension. It has been changing in recent years as the government has equalised the ages for men and women – and it's likely to be an increasingly later age for those who are today in their 40s or younger. The state pension will be a vital part of your planning and Chapter Nine is dedicated to this subject.

## 10. Fund

A fund is a pool of cash or other investments. But in the context of pensions, the word usually describes a ready-made portfolio of investments in which savers can buy units or shares. The portfolios are generally managed by specialist firms known as fund managers or asset managers, examples of which include Fidelity, Invesco, Schroders and Jupiter. The funds pool savers' cash and invest it in shares, bonds, property and other assets according to their objectives. An investment you make in these funds gives you exposure to the mix of underlying investments selected by the fund manager.

# Chapter Two
# Gain Control of Your Pension Pots

### "Where is my pension money?"

IN THE LAST CHAPTER, WE saw that people will increasingly be part of defined contribution workplace pension schemes, which will lead to them building up a pension pot, or series of pots, throughout their working lives. As you near retirement, you need to gain control of this situation so that you are able to begin to manage it.

In this chapter, we outline what you need to do if, like many people, you have a variety of pension plans in different places, perhaps because you worked in the past for several employers that offered a pension scheme, or because you have started various private pension plans. It's time to combine all of these into a single pension pot, which throughout the chapter we refer to as amalgamating your separate pension pots.

It's also important not to forget ISAs or other savings arrangements. These too can contribute to your retirement income. We'll explain how you can deal with these other vehicles in combination with pension plans in this chapter.

You may want to skip this chapter if you already have your retirement savings in one place and are happy to stay with the platform or provider where these savings are held. However, even if this is you, you might benefit from reading the section on choosing a platform

(Step 3), as you may be able to save money or get a better service by switching to another company.

## Pulling it all together

What follows is a seven-step checklist for moving your disparate pots of savings into one amalgamated account ready for you to invest with a view to producing your retirement income. The steps are:

1.  Establish what you have.

2.  Check whether there is any reason to keep any of your existing pensions where they are, either temporarily or permanently.

3.  Choose the platform where you will hold your amalgamated pension pot.

4.  Establish the costs involved, if any, in transferring your money.

5.  Choose whether to transfer your investments as they are, or as cash.

6.  Move your money to your chosen platform.

7.  Almost there...

*Let's work through each of these steps in turn.*

At the end of the seven steps, we have included an example of how this process may look in practice.

We should point out that you can carry out these steps at any age; you do not need to wait until you are about to retire or even until you are 55, the age at which you can start to withdraw money from a pension. However, in a few special circumstances, which we explain below, it will be better to leave your money where it is for now.

Before we get to the seven steps, it is worth taking a moment to explain why we are going through this process of combining pension pots at all.

## Why combine your pension pots?

In this chapter, and indeed the whole book, we assume that you want to combine any discrete pension pots you have built up into a single pot at the point of retirement or before (with some exceptions – see Step 2 below).

The advantage of combining your pension pots is that administration and keeping track of your money will be much easier. It could also be less costly, depending on how the companies involved set their fees.

However, if you decide that you would rather keep your pension pots separate, you can still follow the steps below and in the rest of the book, simply applying everything to each pot individually rather than to the single combined pot.

And now, on to the seven steps.

## Step 1: Establish what you have

It's not unusual to lose track of old pensions and ISAs – even when large sums are involved. Overlooking one of your pensions could mean needlessly settling for a reduced retirement income, so some diligent thought and action at this stage is needed to avoid making this mistake.

First, company pensions. Write a list of all the employers you've ever worked for and try to recall if each offered a pension scheme. If in doubt, assume that they did until proved otherwise.

Now contact the pensions department of each firm to ask for details of their pension scheme. In cases where you are not sure if you had a pension, ask if you were a member of their scheme. Many companies ran multiple schemes at different times or for different categories of employee, so make sure that any information the firm provides relates specifically to the scheme to which you belonged (you may have belonged to more than one).

This step can involve a lot of work, particularly when you are dealing with companies you left decades ago. Some may have gone out of business, changed name or been taken over – perhaps several times. Internet research can help in establishing what happened in each case.

But the important point is that, even when a firm has gone bust, if you built up a pension entitlement it has not gone away. Someone somewhere will be managing a pot of money with your name on it, or will be responsible for paying you most if not all of your promised retirement income – you just need to find out who. The only exception to this is in the case of some defined benefit pensions from companies that went bust many years ago, as we explain in a moment.

If your own research reaches a dead end you can enlist help from a number of sources. For defined benefit pensions, try the Pension Protection Fund (PPF), which takes over the pension schemes of companies that have gone bust. There is a list of all company pension schemes that have been taken over by the PPF since November 2006 on its website (www.tinyurl.com/jtxemlz); you can also contact the PPF via www.pensionprotectionfund.org.uk or 0330 123 2222.

If you were once a member of a scheme that got into trouble before the PPF was able to assist, which means before 5 April 2005, you may be entitled to help from another source of protection called the Financial Assistance Scheme. This, broadly speaking, will pay or top up the pensions of people who belonged to final salary schemes that began to be wound up between January 1997 and April 2005. For more information, see: www.ppf.co.uk/what-it-means-fas.

Only those who had defined benefit pension entitlements more than 20 years ago and haven't checked up on their benefits in that time could find that they have no pension entitlement from that scheme.

Another source of information about potentially forgotten defined benefit pensions is the National Insurance Contribution Office (www.tinyurl.com/ocjexoh). The NIC Office can help if your pension was contracted out of National Insurance, which means that NI contributions were diverted to the pension scheme, reducing your entitlement to top-up state pensions such as SERPS. If in doubt about this point, you should try this service anyway.

If neither of these organisations is able to help, try the government's pension tracing service (www.gov.uk/find-pension-contact-details). This covers all types of pension scheme, including private pensions that you set up yourself without the involvement of an employer.

The Pensions Advisory Service has more useful information on this subject on its website (www.tinyurl.com/jday583) and you can also contact the service on 0300 123 1047.

For private pensions, or for ISAs and other plans, try to remember which companies you used and contact them or their successor firms. Alternatively, use the government's pension tracing service mentioned above.

The phone numbers and web addresses listed may change in future, but a Google search should be useful in such cases.

Once you know how to contact all your old pension schemes, ask each one how much money you have saved there, or, in the case of defined benefit plans, how much entitlement you have built up and what benefits you will receive.

Make a note of all this information using a spreadsheet, or a notepad if you prefer, so that you can refer to it again when you need to. The new *pensions dashboard*, a government initiative, should also help savers to track down old pensions.

## Step 2: Check whether there is any reason to keep any of your old pensions where they are, either temporarily or permanently

This is a vitally important step: getting it wrong here could mean missing out on hugely valuable benefits already earned. In certain cases it could mean paying a huge fee for the privilege of moving your money when such a fee could be avoided simply by delaying the move for a few years.

While the main idea of this book is that you bring all your pension assets together in one place, there are a few cases where this is not the best idea and money should be left where it is, either temporarily or indefinitely.

This is because some pensions, especially those started some time ago, come with valuable perks that will disappear if you transfer the money elsewhere. Before you move any pension assets, check whether your existing plans offer any of the following benefits.

### 1. Final salary benefits

If any of your old pensions is a final salary or defined benefit type, it will almost always be best to stick with it – you will almost certainly get a guaranteed risk-free income that rises every year in line with inflation and which is partially transferred to your spouse if you die first.

However, it is often possible to swap final salary benefits for a cash lump sum (the main exceptions are unfunded public sector schemes, which means most except those run by local authorities). The sums paid can be generous – in some cases in mid-2017, private sector employers were offering 40 times the promised annual pension to those who wanted to leave the scheme – so you may feel that you will be able to generate a higher income from such a sum than you would get under the terms of the pension. However, you would be giving up the guaranteed income for life.

This is an area where advice from an expert is probably needed (and is often required by law in any case). At the very least, think extremely carefully before giving up final salary entitlements.

### 2. Guaranteed annuity rates

The idea of pension money is to generate an income. This book exists partly because the traditional way to get income from a pension pot – an annuity – now pays pitiful rates of return, as we saw in Chapter One. But if you are offered an annuity that delivers an attractive income, it makes sense to take it. The investment ideas we offer later in the book are, we believe, among the safest ways to get income from pensions. But they are not guaranteed, whereas annuity payments are guaranteed.

Some old pension policies offer a guaranteed annuity rate (GAR). Ask the providers of all your defined contribution pensions whether any of them offers a GAR and, if so, request full details of the rate and any conditions attached to it.

Deciding whether a particular rate is worth taking is not straightforward and you may be better off seeking help from a financial adviser who specialises in pensions. Once again, think very carefully before exiting this kind of arrangement and giving up a GAR.

As a rule of thumb, you should at least seek an annuity quote on the open market, which will require you to give your age and details of any medical conditions that could affect your longevity. Then compare these quotes with the GAR to see if the GAR is a significantly better deal.

Check also whether a GAR deal can offer options such as payments for a surviving spouse, or payments that rise each year; sometimes such enhancements are not available in conjunction with GARs.

Finally, some GARs are available only on certain dates, such as the retirement date specified on your policy, so check for any such conditions.

### 3. Minimum values at maturity

In a similar vein, some pension plans guarantee that they will have a certain minimum value at maturity. These guarantees were typically offered on *with-profits* pensions from certain companies around 20 years ago. Look for the term *guaranteed sum assured* or *guaranteed maturity value* on documents relating to the pension. Because expected returns were so much higher in the past, such benefits could be hugely valuable.

Some policies offered guaranteed minimum annual increases as an alternative.

If you are not sure whether your policy included these or other guarantees, or if you cannot find the relevant paperwork, ask the company where the pension is held: "Are there any guarantees of any type on my policy?"

If you do hold a pension with these kinds of guarantees, it may well be worth holding on to them until maturity rather than transferring the money to your amalgamated pot. The decision will depend on how much the guarantees would improve on the current value of the plan (which you can request from the company concerned) and how long you have to wait until maturity. Expert advice may be worthwhile (see Chapter Eleven).

### 4. With-profits pensions that expect to pay big bonuses at maturity

*With-profits* describes a type of investment that was offered to pension savers in the past but is now much less common. The value of the investment is protected to some extent from the ups and downs of the financial markets and tends to rise each year through the award of annual bonuses. Often a terminal bonus is added when the policy matures, which may be some years in the future.

With-profits plans vary widely. A few are well run, such as those from Prudential, Aviva and Legal & General. However, many with-profits plans have not been well run in the past and cannot be expected to pay big bonuses in future.

Determining whether your with-profits plan has been well run in the past, and is therefore worth keeping, is not always easy. We suggest that you consider the following indicators.

First, does the company still offer with-profits policies to new customers or is it closed to new business and only involved in managing plans taken out in the past? The former category is preferable, because a firm is more likely to attract new customers if it is producing good returns for its current ones.

Second, find out how the with-profits plans are invested. You want at least 50% to be in shares. Some have most of their money in bonds and cash, which have less scope to rise in value over the long term.

Finally, look at the bonuses being paid on your policy. With-profits returns are generally based on two bonuses: annual bonuses, which are often guaranteed; and terminal bonuses, which aren't guaranteed. Many with-profits funds are paying small annual bonuses, or none at all, and are relying mostly on terminal bonuses, which means there is less security and more risk of volatile returns. In other words, you want a plan with a good record of guaranteed annual bonuses.

Plans that fail these tests may be worth cashing in so that you can transfer the money to your new amalgamated pot. Ask the company whether any penalties (or so-called market value adjustments, which would reduce the value of your fund) apply before you do this.

## 5. Huge exit penalties

Some pension firms charge extremely large fees if you want to move your money to another company. Friends Life and Abbey Life have sometimes charged 40% of the total value of your savings, for example.

The exact figure will depend on when the policy was taken out and how long it has to run before it matures. In some circumstances the fee could be more like 5%, for example.

But there is an easy way to avoid paying a very high charge to move your money. Under rules introduced in 2017, once you reach the age of 55, the pension firm has to cap its exit charge at just 1%. If you discover that any of your old policies carries a large exit penalty, it is likely to be best simply to wait until you reach 55 before you transfer your money. However, the cap does not apply to the reductions (called market value adjustments) that insurers and pension companies apply when you want to leave a with-profits saving plan. This is dealt with in more detail in Step 4, on page 40.

## 6. Fee amnesties on specific dates

This is a strange feature of some old policies, usually with-profits plans. As mentioned above, some pension providers impose fees if you decide to move your money elsewhere before the plan's maturity date. But even when such fees apply, the firms sometimes offer to waive them on particular dates, often the anniversary of the plan's commencement.

It's a case of looking through the plan documents thoroughly (or asking an adviser to do so) and establishing whether you have any of these get-out-of-jail-free cards. If the amnesty is a long way in the future, you may decide that it's better to pay up now and move the money. It's a question of how long you'd have to wait and the performance you can expect from the plan in the meantime.

Again, specialist help from a financial adviser may be needed before moving your money out of a scheme that carries exit fees.

# Step 3: Choose the firm where you will hold your amalgamated pension pot

You have now decided which of your pension pots you wish to keep as they are and which you wish to transfer into a single place.

Before you can ask the firms that hold your old pension plans to transfer the money to one amalgamated pot, you need to choose the firm where that amalgamated pot will be held and open a new account with that firm. These firms are known by a wide variety of names: you may see them referred to as investment platforms, fund shops, fund supermarkets, or SIPP firms – a SIPP being a self-invested personal pension. We have chosen to use the term platform in this book.

SIPP is a key term if you are going to run your own pension along the lines described in this book. The new account you open for your amalgamated pot will almost certainly be called a SIPP.

Time spent choosing the right SIPP platform will be well rewarded later: if you are drawing income in retirement for 20 or 30 years, even small differences in costs will begin to add up to a sizeable sum. You will also be interacting with your chosen firm fairly frequently, so you want one that is efficient and which offers good customer service.

And you want a firm that will stay the course: the danger of a very cheap firm is that it may not be a sustainable business and it may be forced to put up its prices or sell out to a competitor. These scenarios could mean you paying more and reopen the question of whether you are with the right platform, which is something you would ideally want to avoid.

In summary: you are looking for a reputable, reliable and stable firm, with low fees and costs, and an excellent record for customer service.

How can you identify the ideal platform for you? We are offering two options. The first involves us, the authors, doing most of the work and suggesting a specific platform for you. The second involves you, the reader, undertaking your own research and deciding for yourself which platform is best. This will take longer, but will give you the reassurance that no shortcuts have been taken and that you really have identified the best choice.

## Method 1: Using the platform that we have chosen

We asked a specialist consultancy called The Lang Cat (www. langcatfinancial.co.uk) to analyse the pricing structure of all the major platforms to determine which was likely to be cheapest, taking into account the composition of the portfolios and the pattern of withdrawals involved. Both of these factors significantly affect the amount you will have to pay the platform each year in fees. We then looked at the cheapest options identified by The Lang Cat and used our own knowledge of the industry to identify a platform that could be expected to provide good service, offer the right range of investments and be around for the long term.

**Interactive Investor came out on top**. This is one of the larger and more established platforms. It is not the very cheapest platform in all circumstances, but is among the lowest-cost for the approach we are using and for the sums of money that most people will be investing.

We appreciate that some people will already have their money with a particular platform and may not wish to change. For larger portfolios The Share Centre would be fine as an alternative to Interactive Investor. At the lower end (portfolios of up to about £50,000) Hargreaves Lansdown or AJ Bell Youinvest would suit most investors.

### Method 2: Conduct your own thorough research into finding the best platform

If you would rather carry out your own research into identifying the ideal platform for your circumstances, follow these five steps.

### 1. How does the platform measure up on fees and costs?

As mentioned above, small differences in costs will begin to add up to a sizeable sum over decades. For an illustration of this, take a look at the chart below.

We have assumed that a saver has £300,000 to start with and, for simplicity's sake, that there are no investment gains or losses – and that only the "natural yield", such as the dividends, is taken as income. If annual charges are 1.5% (grey bars) the pot diminishes far more quickly than if they are 1.25% (black bars).

**Chart 2.1: The corrosive effect of fees over time**

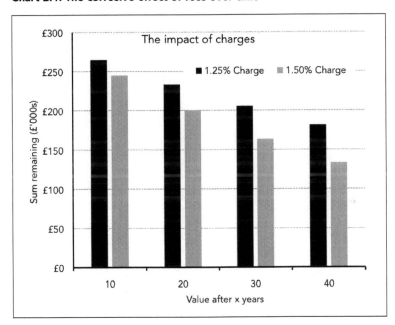

Note: £300,000 initial sum, no investment gains or losses, only natural yield taken. Source: www.comparefundplatforms.com.

*Now that you understand the importance of keeping fees low, you need to compare the fees of the various platforms.*

To compare fees and costs, we favour an easy-to-use price comparison tool put together by The Lang Cat (www.langcatfinancial.co.uk). The tools are tables that show which platforms are most and least expensive according to the size of your pension pot.

The tables assume that you have invested your pension money as suggested in one of the three portfolios in the next chapter. The first table is for the high-income and compromise portfolios; the second is for the inheritance portfolio. The tables also take into account any fees charged to withdraw your money in line with the strategy outlined in Chapter Five. Simply check the appropriate table and look at the column that corresponds to the amount that you will invest.

**Table 2.1: Total annual charges for the high-income and compromise portfolios**

| Platform | £5,000 | £15,000 | £25,000 | £50,000 | £100,000 | £250,000 | £500,000 | £1,000,000 |
|---|---|---|---|---|---|---|---|---|
| AJ Bell Youinvest | £278 | £303 | £328 | £388 | £451 | £638 | £826 | £1,076 |
| Bestinvest | £315 | £345 | £375 | £450 | £468 | £918 | £1,418 | £2,418 |
| Charles Stanley Direct | £389 | £406 | £424 | £507 | £682 | £1,207 | £1,687 | £2,187 |
| Close Brothers A.M. Self Directed Service | £144 | £169 | £194 | £257 | £382 | £757 | £1,382 | £2,632 |
| Fidelity Personal Investing* | £45 | £46 | £77 | £154 | £273 | £548 | £630 | £1,170 |
| Halifax Share Dealing | £580 | £580 | £580 | £580 | £580 | £580 | £580 | £580 |
| Hargreaves Lansdown | £118 | £163 | £208 | £321 | £546 | £1,058 | £1,454 | £2,079 |
| Interactive Investor | £440 | £440 | £440 | £440 | £440 | £440 | £440 | £440 |
| iWeb | £340 | £340 | £340 | £340 | £340 | £340 | £340 | £340 |
| The Share Centre | £474 | £474 | £474 | £474 | £474 | £474 | £474 | £474 |
| Willis Owen | £90 | £150 | £210 | £360 | £560 | £935 | £1,310 | £2,060 |

*At the time of writing Fidelity Personal Investing did not allow investment trusts to be held in its SIPP, so it would not be possible to use Fidelity for the portfolios in this book. However, Fidelity said it hoped to offer investment trusts within SIPPs in the near future.

**Table 2.2: Total annual charges for the inheritance portfolio**

| Platform | £5,000 | £15,000 | £25,000 | £50,000 | £100,000 | £250,000 | £500,000 | £1,000,000 |
|---|---|---|---|---|---|---|---|---|
| AJ Bell Youinvest | £346 | £371 | £394 | £426 | £488 | £676 | £988 | £1,238 |
| Bestinvest | £375 | £405 | £435 | £510 | £528 | £978 | £1,478 | £2,478 |
| Charles Stanley Direct | £457 | £477 | £512 | £599 | £774 | £1,102 | £1,539 | £2,039 |
| Close Brothers A.M. Self Directed Service | £216 | £241 | £266 | £328 | £453 | £828 | £1,453 | £2,703 |
| Fidelity Personal Investing* | £46 | £47 | £78 | £138 | £230 | £508 | £595 | £1,145 |
| Halifax Share Dealing | £580 | £580 | £580 | £580 | £580 | £580 | £580 | £580 |
| Hargreaves Lansdown | £214 | £259 | £304 | £416 | £616 | £954 | £1,516 | £2,141 |
| Interactive Investor | £440 | £440 | £440 | £440 | £440 | £440 | £440 | £440 |
| iWeb | £340 | £340 | £340 | £340 | £340 | £340 | £340 | £340 |
| The Share Centre | £474 | £474 | £474 | £474 | £474 | £474 | £474 | £474 |
| Willis Owen | £150 | £210 | £270 | £420 | £620 | £995 | £1,370 | £2,120 |

*At the time of writing Fidelity Personal Investing did not allow investment trusts to be held in its SIPP, so it would not be possible to use Fidelity for the portfolios in this book. However, Fidelity said it hoped to offer investment trusts within SIPPs in the near future.

The important point is that no single platform is cheapest in all circumstances; it depends heavily on how much money you have in your pot. It also depends on the type of investments you own and how often you intend to change them. This should not be too much of a consideration for those investors who follow our model portfolios, however, because we have selected a limited number of holdings, including both unit and investment trusts, which you would not expect to be trading regularly.

If, however, you want to be absolutely sure that you have the cheapest provider, you may need to do some sums yourself, based on your exact needs. Alternatively, other tools do exist online. One is www.comparefundplatforms.com, although this doesn't take account of the fees involved in withdrawing money from your pension.

## 2. Does the platform offer the range of investments you need?

It may be hard for you to answer this at the moment, although later chapters should help. The most important investment categories are funds and shares. Almost all platforms offer funds, although several do not offer shares. The majority deal in both. Our three portfolios outlined in Chapter Four each have a mixture of funds and shares.

This is not because our approach involves investing in the shares of individual businesses. In fact, we have avoided this approach because it requires a high level of research and monitoring. Instead, we invest exclusively in funds run by professional investors; it just happens that some of the 'funds' we have chosen (namely the investment trusts, explained in Chapter Four) are technically regarded as shares.

Bearing in mind that several well-regarded platforms do offer both types of asset, and that even if you want to restrict yourself to one or other at the moment, things could change in future, it's best to choose a platform that offers both shares and funds.

3. Does the platform allow you to withdraw money in the way that you want at a reasonable price?

Most investment platforms were established before George Osborne's pension freedoms were announced. They were forced to decide quickly how or whether to charge for withdrawals made under the freedoms. The process is still bedding in.

Ideally you want to be able to access your pension money in the way promised by the government when the pension freedoms were announced: just as if you were using a bank account. So you may want to make regular or ad-hoc withdrawals as often as you like, in some cases using methods that minimise your tax bill (these methods are described in Chapter Seven).

You don't want to be caught by unexpected charges for any of these services. The following table sets out what the main platforms charge in this area at the time of writing. These figures are not static and could change. These charges are accounted for in the tables above, assuming that you follow the system of quarterly withdrawals described in Chapter Five, but you may find it useful to know them if you make additional withdrawals.

**Table 2.3: Costs of pension withdrawals**

| Provider | Charge for pension withdrawals |
|---|---|
| **Hargreaves Lansdown** | No charge |
| **AJ Bell Youinvest** | £120 a year, with a further £30 per ad-hoc income payment |
| **Interactive Investor** | £120 a year |
| **Fidelity** | No charge |
| **Charles Stanley Direct** | £60 a year, with a further £30 per ad-hoc income payment (also £180 every time you take some tax-free cash) |
| **Bestinvest** | £120 a year (if SIPP below £100,000), with a further £30 per ad-hoc income payment for all SIPP values |

Source: www.comparefundplatforms.com

## 4. Usability

If you find a particular platform's website hard to use, you may be put off from carrying out important tasks. It's worth taking a look around the website of the platform you are thinking of choosing before you make a final decision.

Standards of telephone support also vary and some platforms (typically cheaper ones) are online-only operations. Try phoning the companies to see how quickly they answer the phone and how responsive they are to some simple questions about their services. If a firm passes this test, it's a good sign.

Look also at the range of research and analytical tools offered on the website, which is something else that varies widely.

## 5. Financial strength and reputation

The chance of losing any of your pension investments through the failure of a platform, or through administrative incompetence, is very small. These firms are tightly regulated and your assets belong legally to you, irrespective of the financial state of the firm that administers them.

If your platform went bust, you would keep all your assets. (A very small number of investors did lose money when a minor platform called Beaufort Securities went bust in 2018. There were special circumstances involved; we believe the chances of similar losses at one of the big platforms are extremely small.) However, even if your money is safe, having it with a platform that fails is very much something to be avoided, as administrative headaches and delays would be very likely. It's hard to say for sure whether you would be able to continue making withdrawals while things were sorted out – and these withdrawals are your income!

You don't really want to get involved in trying to assess the financial strength of a pension platform, but we can say that the vast majority of the best and most popular platforms are either very large, successful businesses in their own right, or are part of much larger financial institutions such as banks or fund groups. It is unlikely any of these will fall into financial difficulties.

Reputation is also important: firms that have a high public profile will want to avoid the adverse publicity that disgruntled customers can generate by taking complaints to the media. Accordingly, they tend to be more inclined to nip problems in the bud. The best known platforms include Hargreaves Lansdown, Barclays Smart Investor (formerly Barclays Stockbrokers), Fidelity Personal Investing, AJ Bell Youinvest, Halifax Share Dealing and Interactive Investor.

The final point is that solid, profitable platforms are less likely to increase their prices suddenly or to be sold to a rival. Both types of disruption are best avoided from your point of view.

Maintain a keen focus on costs, but weigh this against all the other factors. Keep everything under annual review and be prepared to switch if changing circumstances make it essential. It may be worth deciding in advance which platform would be your backup choice.

However, switching is not to be undertaken lightly. The costs and inconvenience involved can be considerable and the process can take a long time – often many months – to complete. You would need to be prepared financially for such disruption, perhaps by withdrawing the equivalent of several months' income before the switch.

---

## I have accounts with 28 pension firms – these six are the best

**Holly Mackay** set up her business Boring Money with the sole purpose to scrutinise Britain's investment platforms. As part of the process, she opened accounts with 28 of them in her own name so that she could assess their usability and reliability. We asked her to review six of the best.

## Hargreaves Lansdown

"These guys dominate the field and are very good. For busy people who just want things to work, the service is unbeatable. Good service costs, however: they are at the pricey end with an administration fee starting at 0.45% a year. But this FTSE 100 giant offers security, peace of mind and slick service. Very good."

Boring Money customer ratings (out of 5): 209 reviews

Value: 3.3

Website: 4.4

Service: 4.2

## Barclays Smart Investor

"At the time of writing this service had just undergone a metamorphosis. The original service, Barclays Stockbrokers, was great for traders and those who wanted detailed research. But the revamped offering has been either simplified or dumbed down, according to who you listen to. Could be handy for those who bank with Barclays and want a simple solution that fits into other parts of their financial lives."

Boring Money customer ratings (out of 5): 28 reviews

Value: 2.3

Website: 2.2

Service: 2.2

## Interactive Investor

"This business acquired a rival, TD Direct, and the services were merged at the end of 2017, which led to some disruption. Interactive's fixed-fee structure has been implemented for all former TD customers, which makes this platform a very good deal for those with £50,000 or more. Service and website usability have been patchy in the past, but developments on the pension front and general upgrades should improve things steadily."

Boring Money customer ratings (out of 5): 39 reviews

Value: 4.3

Website: 3.3

Service: 3.5

## Fidelity

"A decently priced big-brand offering, which has recently improved its website and ease of use. The service and staff on the phones are good. One problem has been the lack of well integrated share dealing, which would affect readers of this book because the three portfolios include investment trusts, which are a special type of share. We expect Fidelity to improve this aspect in the future. A smooth journey for those who want some help and signposting. On the up."

Boring Money customer ratings (out of 5): 64 reviews

Value: 3.5

Website: 3.5

Service: 3.6

## AJ Bell Youinvest

"Consistently at the low-cost end, whether you have a large or small portfolio. It's more suited to confident investors and can confuse beginners. These guys certainly know pensions and I think are ones to watch."

Boring Money customer ratings (out of 5): 83 reviews

Value: 3.8

Website: 3.8

Service: 3.9

## Charles Stanley Direct

"A low-cost platform that might be a bit overwhelming for novice investors. But it's getting better and is hard to beat on cost, especially for smaller portfolios."

Boring Money customer ratings (out of 5): 22 reviews

Value: 4.4

Website: 3.9

Service: 4.2

---

# Step 4: Establish the costs involved, if any, in transferring your money

As we mentioned above, some pension schemes may charge fees to move money to another firm. Some charges depend on the exact circumstances, such as those that apply if the policy has not yet matured, while others are simply administrative fees.

The fees may come by various names and may not be immediately obvious for what they are. For example, with-profits policies may apply a *market value adjustment* (MVA) if you want your money before maturity.

A market value adjustment is a roundabout way of telling you that your investment has gone down in value. It's a classic case of investment firms – insurers, in this case – using unnecessary jargon to hide the bad news.

Your policy value will appear as usual on your regular statement. This won't necessarily show any fall in the underlying investments. The latter will only become apparent if you want to cash out of your policy, in which case the MVA will suddenly apply. Thankfully these types of with-profits policies are disappearing.

Weigh up whether an MVA is worth paying, or if it's better, in view of the policy's prospects, to wait until you can transfer without cost. It's not possible to give hard and fast guidance about how to do this, but if a lot of money is at stake it may be worth getting advice. Otherwise, it may be best to leave the plan alone if there is a large MVA and wait for the policy to mature before transferring the money.

Company pensions and the more modern personal pensions, which tend not to be of the with-profits type, are unlikely to impose charges large enough to make moving your money unwise. They may charge some kind of administrative or other fee for exiting.

*What about fees imposed by your new pension company for joining?*

While a few firms charge for setting up a new pension plan, most do not. Some even encourage you to switch to them by covering the transfer fees imposed by your previous pension firm, so it is worth asking about that.

## Step 5: Choose whether to transfer your investments as they are, or as cash

When you transfer your pension pots, you may be given the option of taking your money in cash or transferring the actual investments as they are. The latter option is known as an *in specie transfer*. There are advantages and disadvantages of each method.

Transferring the money as cash, which will mean selling the investments first, transferring the cash, and then making new investments with your new provider, will sometimes be cheaper. It is almost bound to be quicker and less prone to administrative hiccups.

On the other hand, if you plan to reinvest in broadly the same assets within your new amalgamated pension, you are exposed to the risk that the market climbs sharply while your money is in cash and you are making the transfer, meaning that you miss out on the gain. An in specie transfer will guard against this risk.

That said, we suspect most people will probably prefer to make the transfer in cash, because your self-managed investment strategy (see Chapter Four) is likely to be tailor-made to new circumstances in retirement. It will therefore require a different range of holdings to those in which the pension pot was invested during your working life.

## Step 6: Move your money to the new firm

This isn't quite as simple as writing to the firms involved and requesting a transfer. Accordingly, expect the process to take time, perhaps some weeks, and plan appropriately.

You will need to have the account at your new firm set up. The old providers are likely to check that you know what you are doing, so they may ask if you have taken advice or to certify that you are aware of the risks involved in managing your investments.

Firms will normally require written instructions in the post.

Once all these requests have been sent, you should monitor progress and chase any firms that drag their heels.

---

## What about your ISAs?

This chapter describes what you should do if you have saved money in pension plans, but many people also have money in ISAs – or have used ISAs exclusively and avoided pensions. This book is intended to be equally useful for those savers.

There are technical differences between ISAs and pension plans. If you do hold money in ISAs you may need to take some different steps in order to make the most of it when it comes to generating retirement income.

### Cash ISAs

These simple savings plans are extremely popular and most people probably have one or more cash ISAs. How can you best use them as part of your wider strategy for generating retirement income?

A lot depends on how much you have in cash ISAs. As we will explain in Chapter Four, you should keep a substantial sum in cash – enough to cover your normal income needs for at least a year.

If you have that kind of sum in cash ISAs already, it will probably make sense to leave those ISAs exactly as they are. If you have more than that in cash, however, it will be best to invest the excess in income-producing assets. This can be done in exactly the way we describe in Chapter Four.

If you have less than a year's worth of income in cash ISAs, we would suggest leaving them as they are, but ensuring that some of your pension savings are kept in cash too, to bring the total up to the target level. Alternatively, if you also have stocks & shares ISAs, you could transfer some of that money into cash ISAs (we explain more about ISA transfers below).

## Stocks & shares ISAs

The simplest way to handle any stocks & shares ISAs is to leave them in place, but invest the money as described in Chapter Four. Manage withdrawals from your ISAs in conjunction with your pension withdrawals as we describe in Chapter Five to ensure that you don't run down your money too quickly.

## Moving money from cash ISAs to stocks & shares ISAs (and vice versa)

Be careful when moving money in stocks & shares ISAs to cash ISAs, or vice versa. The rules stipulate that, in order to keep the tax benefits, you should transfer directly from one type of ISA to the other rather than withdrawing money from the old ISA, holding the money in your bank account for a short while, and then putting it into a new ISA.

Making the transfer in the right way is easy. Let's say you want to move some of the money in your cash ISAs to a stocks & shares ISA in order to invest it in the income-producing assets we outline later.

First, choose the company that you want to administer your stocks & shares ISA (it will probably be simplest to use the same one that you chose to manage your amalgamated pension pot; alternatively, you could follow the same process described in step 3 of this chapter for choosing a pension provider).

Then, ask this company to contact your cash ISA provider on your behalf and transfer the sum you specify. The new provider should handle the whole process and the money will appear in your stocks & shares ISA within a week or so, ready for you to invest it.

For transfers from stocks & shares ISAs to cash ISAs, the process is similar: contact the provider of the ISA to which you want the money transferred and the process will be managed on your behalf.

## Two tax tricks that allow you to get more from ISAs

If you have saved for retirement in both pensions and ISAs, a couple of opportunities for minimising your tax bill, or augmenting your savings pot via tax relief, spring up. Taking advantage of these opportunities can be complex, however.

The first arises from the fact that when you pay money into a pension, tax relief is added on top. This in effect boosts the amount you pay into the pension by 25% for basic-rate taxpayers, or 67% for higher-rate taxpayers. This perk applies to money taken out of ISAs and put into a pension, just as it does to money taken from, for example, your salary.

If you withdraw, say, £10,000 from a cash ISA and pay it into a pension, the company that administers the pension will automatically claim £2,500 from HMRC on your behalf and add it to the pension, taking the total to £12,500. This is because, as a basic-rate taxpayer, you would have paid £2,500 in income tax on £12,500.

Higher-rate taxpayers can claim back a further £2,500 via their tax return. If this tax rebate is taken into account, they effectively pay a net £7,500 for a pension contribution of £12,500 (the 67% boost we referred to a moment ago).

This may sound like an amazing offer of free money from the taxman, but there are a couple of points to bear in mind.

First, the rules are complex, so tread carefully. Ensure that you don't exceed the annual limit for pension contributions (£40,000, or £10,000 for higher earners – those who earn £150,000 or more per year), or the lifetime allowance for total pension savings (£1.055m in 2019–20). You can use the previous three years' annual allowances if they were not fully used at the time.

Also, the tax relief you get when you pay money into a pension is partly offset by the fact that withdrawals from pensions are taxable, whereas withdrawals from ISAs are not. The upshot of this is that, if you are a basic-rate taxpayer when you contribute to the pension and still a basic-rate taxpayer when you withdraw the money in retirement, the only benefit is the 25% lump sum that everyone can take from their pension tax-free.

The biggest benefit of transferring money from an ISA to a pension is reserved for those who pay the higher rate of tax when they pay the money into the pension, but only the basic rate when they come to withdraw the money in retirement. If you think you are in this situation, transferring ISA money to a pension while you are still a higher-rate taxpayer deserves serious consideration.

If you decide to leave your ISAs as they are, you do have an opportunity to save tax in retirement, particularly if you plan to leave a sizeable legacy to your children. What you do is take as much of your retirement income as you can from your ISAs, leaving as much of your pension as possible untouched. The withdrawals from your ISAs are tax-free, so you may be able to take your total income over, for example, the threshold for higher-rate tax and still pay only the basic rate that particular year.

Then, when you die, the untouched money in your pension can be passed to your heirs free of inheritance tax, although those who inherit will sometimes have to pay income tax at their own rate on any withdrawals.

## Step 7: Almost there

Now it's just a question of ensuring that all your instructions have been carried out by the companies involved.

When all your old pension schemes have acted on your requests, check that every penny has arrived at your new platform. Remember that the process can be slow. Do the same with any ISA switches, which tend to be much quicker.

If you did deliberately leave some money in an old pension scheme or schemes, perhaps to await a fee amnesty on a specific date in the future, or because you are waiting for a with-profits policy to mature, make a diary note of the date concerned or send instructions in advance, then check that the firm takes the action you requested at the right time.

And that's it – you are now ready to start managing your own pension savings in order to generate the retirement income you need. The next chapters explain how.

## An example of amalgamating pension accounts

Glenn Mousley, 64, is probably typical of many people at about retirement age: he accumulated several pots of savings over the course of his career and now has three pensions, as well as several ISAs.

In some cases he has had to take action to get the most out of his pension savings – but in other cases he has decided it is best to leave some money where it is.

### Pension 1: From final salary to a self-managed SIPP

Early in his career Mr Mousley worked for several years for BOC (British Oxygen Company) and joined the firm's final salary pension scheme. Some years after his departure from BOC, he cashed in this pension: in return for giving up his rights to an index-linked retirement income from the company he was able to take a lump sum and invest it, along with money from another small retirement savings policy, in a pension pot style plan with a company called Target.

"Target was all the rage at the time and for a couple of years my money grew strongly," Mr Mousley said. But it later collapsed and its pension funds were passed on several times to high-charging companies, ending up at Abbey Life. Finally, what was left was moved to an existing plan of Mr Mousley's run by Friends Life, which already contained some other pension savings.

In 2008 he transferred the money again to a SIPP run by Hargreaves Lansdown.

"At that stage I was looking at the whole pension market and assessing my options. SIPPs were quite new then, but by that time I was comfortable with investing in shares and funds," Mr Mousley said.

"One of the problems with the Friends Life pension was that I had no control over how the money was invested. But in a SIPP you had immediate control – your investments could be as risky or as safe as you wanted. I expected to get better returns this way and that has broadly been the case."

He said he had looked at various SIPP companies before he chose Hargreaves Lansdown. "It seemed to have a good record and a straightforward investment process. The transfer was simple and there were no problems. It was quite exciting to get the money there and be able to do what I wanted with it," he said.

### Pension 2: An escape from Equitable Life

Mr Mousley had also saved early in his career in a pension with Equitable Life, the mutual insurer that collapsed in spectacular style in 2001.

As soon as he could, he transferred his savings to a plan with Aviva, although he had to suffer a withdrawal penalty,

"I'm pleased that I did, as things went on to be even worse at Equitable," he said. "At Aviva the investments performed OK. The plan ran until January 2015, at which time I transferred the money to my Hargreaves Lansdown SIPP."

"I filled in an online form on Hargreaves' website and they did everything. I just had to sign an Aviva release form. It was all very easy – the investments at Aviva were sold and the money was moved to Hargreaves as cash. It took about three weeks."

### Pension 3: Left alone – for good reason

Mr Mousley began to save monthly in a pension scheme with Friends Provident around 40 years ago. It was of the pension pot type, so when he decided to take it on his 64th birthday he could have withdrawn the whole sum, using the pension freedoms, or transferred it to Hargreaves Lansdown and amalgamated it with his SIPP there.

However, there was a compelling reason to leave the pension at Friends Provident: it came with a guaranteed annuity rate of 11%. As mentioned earlier in this chapter, such guarantees can be extremely valuable now that annuity rates generally are so low.

"I was always aware that the policy came with a guaranteed annuity rate, but as time went on this aspect became more valuable despite modest performance of the actual investments," Mr Mousley said. "So I realised it was best to leave this pension well alone and I am now receiving the income promised at the 11% rate."

### Some stocks and shares ISAs

Mr Mousley also had some stocks & shares ISAs. These were taken out with a number of fund management companies, including Artemis. When it became beneficial in terms of cost, they were moved to one of three platforms, Hargreaves Lansdown, Aegon (formerly Cofunds) and Fidelity Funds Network. The funds were transferred directly from ISA to ISA, to avoid loss of tax benefits. The fund holdings were not sold, but moved across as is (or *in specie* in industry jargon), to avoid missing out on any investment gains while the transfer took place.

## The outcome

After he took the 25% tax-free lump sum from his SIPP Mr Mousley left the remainder invested in order to produce income.

This pot – from the amalgamation of pensions 1 and 2 – is now worth about £180,000 and he is drawing about £9,000 from it per year.

"I'm broadly happy with the way things have turned out," he said. "There is no one solution that works for everyone, but my view is that if you are reasonably comfortable with the financial markets and with buying and selling investments, the way I have chosen is a good way to go."

# Part Two

## Being Your Own Pension Manager

In Part Two we explain how to begin to invest and manage your pension money. Chapter Three lays out the groundwork, explaining why your assets need to be managed with great care in retirement, and then Chapter Four introduces actual portfolios in which you can invest your money. Chapter Five then sets out in detail how to manage the process of taking the income from your investments.

# Chapter Three
# Making Sure Your Money Lasts as Long as You Do

**"What happens if my pension money's all spent before I die?"**

Now that you have gathered your pension savings together into a single pot, the next step is to consider how long you need that amalgamated pension pot to last. You don't want that pot of money to run out before you die, as this would leave you with no income to pay for life's essentials, let alone luxuries.

## How much can I spend each year?

*"I'm 67, with a £145,000 pension pot. How much can I spend each year?"*

That's what one *Telegraph* reader, let's call her Charlotte, asked in an email. Her question, except for the precise age and sum involved, was like scores of others received each month.

The answer, unfortunately, is somewhat longer than the question. Nor is it conclusive.

In previous chapters, we explained how until recently retirees would in most cases enjoy some certainty around their income. They would be likely to have regular monthly payments either from their final salary pension scheme or from an annuity – or perhaps even both.

Now, though, people like Charlotte arrive at their retirement with a pension pot and some very tricky questions.

How much Charlotte can spend each year is determined by two factors. The first factor relates to investment returns: how much can Charlotte's £145,000 generate by way of returns, even while she is drawing an income from it?

The second factor is longevity. How long is Charlotte going to live?

And in those two issues – both of them unanswerable questions – lies the pension income investor's dilemma in a nutshell.

This dilemma has vexed financial planners, investors and academics for decades. It has been the subject of numerous books, theses and learned discussions. In the end, the solutions that have been thrown up as a result of all this study rely upon looking back at a growing mountain of past data.

What can history tell us about our likely lifespans? What can history tell us about the likely returns on our investments?

## Counting your days on earth

Government actuaries, insurers and other institutions crunch billions of pieces of data in order to try to predict the future. They can put an estimate on the lifespan of someone born today; and they can put an estimate (probably far more accurate) on the remaining lifespan of someone living today, according to their current age.

The following table, which is based on official statistics, effectively sets out the year in which you are going to die. That is provided, of course, that you conform to the historic average.

**Table 3.1: In what year will you die?**

| Your age now | Male? You'll die in... | Female? You'll die in... |
|---|---|---|
| 50 | 2053 aged 86 | 2055 aged 88 |
| 55 | 2047 aged 86 | 2050 aged 88 |
| 60 | 2043 aged 86 | 2045 aged 88 |
| 65 | 2038 aged 86 | 2040 aged 88 |
| 70 | 2034 aged 87 | 2036 aged 89 |
| 75 | 2030 aged 88 | 2031 aged 89 |
| 80 | 2025 aged 89 | 2027 aged 90 |

Source: Historic longevity data extracted from the Office for National Statistics (ONS).

Based on the same statistics as were used to generate the table above, Charlotte is going to die aged 88 years and nine months. Since she was born in 1950, if she conforms to the average she'll die in 2038. That gives her 21 more years from age 67.

In reality, Charlotte is unlikely to conform to the average. She may die next year. Or she may live to be 110, in which case she'll die in 2060 and need her pension income to stretch over 43 years.

This longevity question is the greatest unknown for pension planners, and underestimating likely lifespans has been the financial undoing of countless individuals and businesses. It's something that could, arguably, even wreck the finances of nations as their populations age, drawing expensive state or civil service pensions which were never adequately funded.

Back to your pension pot: what if *you* live to 100, or 110?

That would be a nightmare to budget for.

On the other hand, you do not want to be unnecessarily scrimping and saving in your early retirement when you are fit and energetic, just on the off chance that you might outlive Methuselah.

There is thus a conflict between wanting to give yourself the highest possible income and wanting to make sure your money lasts for an unknown period.

There are effectively two solutions to this conundrum – let's look at what they are.

## Two ways to take income from your pension pot

When you get to the point of using your pension pot to pay yourself an income in retirement, your two basic options are:

1. Take the *natural yield* from your pension investments and use this as your income.

2. Draw your income from a combination of natural yield and gradually selling some of your investments.

We explain these two methods in more detail very shortly, but first it is useful to look at what we mean by natural yield and investment growth.

### Yield and growth – and both

Investment returns are comprised of two components: capital growth and yield.

With a savings account, for example, your capital is entrusted to a bank and you are paid interest in return. This interest can be said to be your yield from placing your cash with the bank.

You get dividends from owning many shares, for example – that's the yield from the shares. But the shares also have a value, and if that rises over time it's referred to as capital growth. With a buy-to-let property the rent you receive as a landlord would be the yield, while any increase in the property's value would be capital growth.

When you buy bonds (or bond funds), each bond represents the loan of your capital to a government or a company. Your yield is in the form of the interest (also called the *coupon*) paid by the bond. Bonds do sometimes increase in value too, giving rise to capital growth.

When we use the term *natural yield* we are describing the income produced by an investment – any investment – as distinct from rises in the value of the investment itself.

With buy-to-let property, the natural yield would be rental income after costs. And where shares are concerned, the dividends are the natural yield. Where the investments are bonds, the interest, or coupon, forms the natural yield.

This brings us to the first of our two solutions mentioned above: living off natural yield.

## Solution 1: Living off the natural yield

If you can manage to live off just the interest earned by your investments, you could leave the capital value untouched. This is known as *living off the natural yield* and for some people it is the ultimate aim.

In real life, however, few people can afford to live off the natural yield of their cash or investments. This is partly because they don't have enough money to start with, and partly because it's difficult to find investments that generate sufficient yield to make it possible.

We are currently living through a period when investment yields are extremely low (see Table 1.1 in Chapter One). This means we pay a high price for assets that produce an income. A strategy based around the objective to live on natural yield alone might, therefore, involve putting money into the small group of investments that do offer high yields – and many of them are too risky.

*Let's look at an example.*

The FTSE 100 index of leading British shares – which includes gigantic companies such as BP, Vodafone and HSBC, which pay generous dividends – yielded around 3.7% at the time of writing.

In other words, for every £1,000 invested across those companies, your dividend payments in a year would be £37 (3.7% of £1,000). To obtain an income of, say, £30,000 per year, you would therefore need to invest £798,000 in a spread of FTSE 100 shares.

Table 3.2 and Chart 3.1 show how much you'd need to invest to obtain a more modest £20,000 annual income from a range of different investments.

**Table 3.2: How much you would need to invest to earn £20,000 per year in natural yield from various assets**

| Asset | Yield | Need to invest |
|-------|-------|----------------|
| **Shares** | 3.7% | £540,000 |
| **Government bonds** | 1.2% | £1.6m |
| **Central London buy-to-let** | 3.2% | £625,000 |
| **Fixed-term cash deposits** | 2.0% | £1m |

**Chart 3.1: How much you would need to invest to earn £20,000 per year in natural yield from various assets**

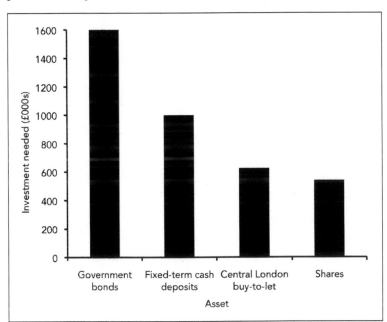

It's quite clear that drawing only natural yield isn't an option for anyone other than the wealthiest of people – and even then it may not be advisable.

Piling all of your money into a single investment in this way (such as £1.6m in government bonds, or £625,000 in buy-to-let property) would be risky, as it would concentrate your portfolio on just one type of asset. As you will see in Chapter Four, it is better to put money into a range of different areas.

There are tax considerations with the natural yield approach, too. Capital growth is taxed differently from income – and in some cases more generously. We look at this in Chapter Seven.

Even so, some people will still want to adopt the strategy of living as much as possible off natural yield. Perhaps they wish to do this because they have a much younger spouse who will need to live off the money for longer, or because they wish to leave capital intact to pass on to children as a legacy.

But the vast majority of savers will need to take the natural yield from their portfolio and, in addition, gradually sell some of the assets in their portfolio as they go. In other words, live off their capital too. This is our second solution.

## Solution 2: Gradually spending some of your capital

Those investors who choose to regularly sell holdings as part of their means to generate income from their pension pot – unlike the natural yield crowd – have to know how much it is safe to sell, and when.

Selling investments means you are saying goodbye to the dividends they will pay in future. That is why selling is such a serious business. Can you really afford to give up that future stream of payments in return for a one-off sum today?

A great deal of statistical analysis has been brought to bear on this problem, and many highly technical solutions have been proposed.

In reality, you are unlikely to want – or to be able to afford – to preserve 100% of your pension pot's value over the course of your retirement.

You will be taking a mix of natural yield, in the form of dividends and interest, and the proceeds of selling investments as you go, and the chances are your pension pot will deplete over time – but in a safe and managed way.

If this all sounds rather daunting and confusing, don't worry.

In Chapter Four we set out a range of model portfolios: one is intended to pay 4% income a year, from natural yield alone; another to pay 5%, from a mixture of natural yield and gradual sales of investments; while the final portfolio, designed for those who want to leave a substantial legacy, should pay 3% from natural yield alone. And in Chapter Five, we explain precisely how you can manage your withdrawals to ensure you're not taking out too much, too fast.

# Chapter Four
# How to Build an Income Portfolio from Scratch

**"How do I choose investments for my pension?"**

Building an income portfolio from scratch is easier than you might think.

The first step towards your income-producing pension pot is already in place: you have transferred all your available pots of money to a platform that is able to provide the service you need.

The next step is a crucial one: to deploy the money in your amalgamated pot into income-producing investments. In this chapter, we guide you through the steps you need to take to build the right income portfolio for your circumstances and present our three model portfolios, one of which should be suitable for you.

## The need for an income portfolio

We now come to what is arguably the heart of this book: the actual investment portfolios into which you will deploy your pension savings in order to generate a secure income that is sufficient to meet your needs in retirement.

In this chapter, we detail three portfolios, each of which contains assets such as shares and bonds, into which your pension money can be invested to produce this income.

But first we briefly explain why it's necessary to take the trouble – and yes, to some extent the risk – of investing in shares and bonds when two seemingly safe options, namely cash accounts and annuities, exist. If you have already decided not to consider either cash or annuities, you can skip these parts.

## Why not cash?

You might be thinking, do I really have to bother running an investment portfolio? Why isn't it an option to simply put your newly amalgamated pension pot into a bank account and let it sit there?

It's true that just keeping all your money in cash, which will pay interest and involve no risk to your capital, is in theory an option. In fact, it would have been a perfectly viable approach in the past – and may indeed become viable again in the future.

But at the moment, with interest rates at record lows, it is not a realistic option unless you have very large sums at your disposal, or if you are so risk-averse that you are prepared to sacrifice a great deal of the income you might otherwise make from a different approach.

To illustrate the extent of the problem, consider a £300,000 pension pot held purely in a cash account. At the time of writing, the highest interest rate you could obtain on this cash is about 1.9%. This rate is available from a special kind of savings account for holding cash within a pension plan. This special type of cash account is needed because pensions have a particular legal status that means the money in them cannot be put into ordinary bank accounts. With that interest rate of 1.9%, you would earn an income of £5,700 a year. Even with the state pension on top, that is probably not enough for you to live on.

And while your capital would appear to remain intact at £300,000 from year to year, it would actually be eroded all the time by inflation. In fact, the current rate of inflation is more than the 1.9% return the account offers on the cash.

The following table shows how the real value of that £300,000 would decline as the years passed with inflation at 2.3%. After 35 years, a not uncommon length of retirement these days, it would be worth just £132,871 in terms of today's purchasing power. The income, if it remained at £5,700 a year, would also lose purchasing power at the same rate.

**Table 4.1: The effect of inflation at 2.3% on the purchasing power of £300,000**

| Time elapsed | Future value of £300,000 |
|---|---|
| 1 year | £293,100 |
| 5 years | £267,051 |
| 10 years | £237,721 |
| 15 years | £211,612 |
| 20 years | £188,370 |
| 25 years | £167,682 |
| 30 years | £149,265 |
| 35 years | £132,871 |

Our model portfolios, by contrast, aim to produce larger incomes. One of the portfolios targets an income of 5%, which would equate to £15,000 on a £300,000 pot. The portfolios may, if markets are favourable, provide capital growth as well.

## And why not annuities?

We have seen that simply putting your money into cash is not an option. But what about an annuity? Wouldn't it just make life easier to buy an annuity and be done with it?

Annuities can offer many advantages. They are guaranteed to pay a given income until you die and this income can, if you choose, rise each year in line with inflation and be paid to your spouse after your death.

Annuities also involve no trouble in later life: you buy one, perhaps at retirement age, and then simply receive the income every month. Choosing the right annuity involves some research, but once you have bought it there is nothing more to do. Our portfolios, by contrast, will need monitoring and sometimes changing – things that are likely to become more troublesome as you age.

We should acknowledge that there is sometimes a place for buying an annuity when you retire and that you might want to at least consider them at this point. In particular, those with impaired life expectancy because of health conditions or lifestyle choices such as smoking may be offered annuity rates sufficiently good to make them worthwhile.

But for most people, the incomes offered by annuities at the point of retirement are simply too low at present. For example, if you want annual increases in your income and for your spouse to benefit if you die, the most you will receive at the time of writing is an annuity rate of 2.8% at age 65, which would mean £8,400 a year from a £300,000 pension pot.

And so, once again, this income of £8,400 from an annuity is unlikely to be enough for you to live on, even with the state pension on top.

In the later stages of retirement we believe that annuities have a key role to play for many, as we will explain in Chapter Six, so we do not disregard them completely.

## That leaves our income portfolios...

It's clear that in the current era of low returns from both cash savings and annuities, many retired people who lack final salary pensions will need to invest their retirement savings pot in an income portfolio to get the income they need. Cash and annuities are not viable options.

Below, you will find our three model income portfolios for retired investors.

You may be wondering why we have suggested three portfolios rather than just one. The answer is that the portfolios have different aims to reflect people's different circumstances and needs.

If you have no children or other close relatives, for example, you can concentrate solely on your own need for income during your life. The aim here may be to use all the money in your pot to fund your retirement and not leave any cash unspent when you die. This is the purpose of our **high-income portfolio**, which targets an annual income of 5% of your initial pension pot, rising with inflation.

If, on the other hand, you are determined to leave a substantial legacy, your portfolio, and the rate at which you make withdrawals, will be different. Our **inheritance portfolio** aims to maintain the value of your assets in real terms while paying an income of 3% of the initial pot, again rising with inflation. This point about maintaining the value of assets in real terms means that the assets retain their buying power after taking account of inflation.

Some people would like to leave a legacy, but not at the expense of their own income in retirement. Our **compromise portfolio**, which stands midway between the other two, is for them; its income target is 4%.

## Using investment funds

In constructing the portfolios, we have used mostly funds. These are professionally managed baskets of shares and other assets. All of the funds we have selected are well-known, mainstream funds and will be available from major platforms.

We have aimed for simplicity and ease of administration, which means keeping the number of funds in each portfolio to a minimum. Nonetheless, we cannot rely on a very small number of funds – such as just one or two – because this would expose the portfolios to the skills and choices of a small number of fund managers.

It's safer to opt for a wider range of funds, to reduce the risk of one manager performing badly. For this reason, as well as to achieve a mix of assets, each portfolio consists of eight holdings.

There are a few admin points you need to understand about funds in order to build the portfolios correctly and feel confident in what you are doing. These points are covered below.

## Why do the portfolios hold funds rather than investing directly?

In theory we could have chosen a basket of shares to invest in directly, rather than investing in funds and leaving the job of choosing individual investments to fund managers. But experience suggests that many find the task of managing a portfolio of shares more daunting than managing funds.

Although the funds we have chosen should be suitable to hold for a very long time, perhaps even for your entire retirement, it would be wise to reassure yourself of their continuing suitability periodically. We explain how to do this in the next chapter, as part of our comprehensive programme for ensuring that your portfolio remains on track.

## Unit trusts, investment trusts and share classes

We have chosen to build our portfolios with two types of fund. The first, which may be called a unit trust, open-ended fund, open-ended investment company, or even just fund, is simply a collection of shares (or other assets, such as bonds) chosen either by a fund manager or by an automated process. The price of a unit in the fund is, put simply, an average of the prices of its component shares (or other assets).

The second type, called an investment trust (or sometimes an investment company or closed-ended fund), is similar – it is also a collection of shares, bonds and other assets. But in this case the fund is structured as a limited company in its own right and the shares in *that* company are listed on the stock market.

There are several other differences between unit trusts and investment trusts, many of which are of little relevance to this book. One important distinction, however, is that platforms will always charge you a fee when you buy or sell an investment trust (for example, Hargreaves Lansdown charges £11.95 and AJ Bell £9.95), whereas many platforms do not charge to buy or sell unit trusts, or charge much less.

We have borne this point in mind in our attempts to identify the most cost-effective platforms and have minimised our use of investment trusts in the high-income portfolio, where regular sales of each holding are envisaged.

As investment trusts are quoted companies, they have a stock market *ticker* symbol, which acts as a unique means of identification. Other funds are identified by name (or with long numbers such as "ISIN" or "SEDOL" numbers). Ordinary funds, as opposed to investment trusts, also tend to come in varieties called "share classes" and sometimes it is important to buy the right class (choosing the wrong one can mean paying extra every year). We have indicated the correct share class where appropriate.

There are often good reasons to choose one type of fund in preference to the other. For example, for our exposure to commercial property we have chosen investment trusts rather than unit trusts. This is because the latter face a problem when it comes to property: investors in a unit trust can ask for their money back at any time, but to raise that money by selling the funds' property assets is likely to take the fund manager many months.

This problem was in evidence after the EU referendum in 2016, when investors turned away from commercial property en masse in fear of a downturn in the UK property market. Almost all the property unit trusts were forced to suspend redemptions as investors tried to get their money out and the funds tried to sell their property assets to fund these requests.

Investment trusts do not face this problem because investors who want their money back have to find another investor to buy their shares. In practice this means selling on the stock market via a stockbroker. This market never dries up, although in periods of turmoil you can expect demand for the property fund's shares, and thus their prices, to fall.

## Passive tracker funds versus active funds

All the funds in our portfolios are run by professional investors employed by fund management firms. But recently another type of fund has made great strides: these are funds that do away with detailed analysis of individual shares and instead simply buy all the stocks in a particular index, such as the FTSE 100. These automated funds are called *tracker* or *passive* funds.

You might imagine that avoiding any attempt at share selection would be foolhardy and would result in a fund that held many unsuitable investments. But the evidence is that many traditional funds fail to do any better than these dumb passive funds, despite the efforts made by their professional managers.

Tracker funds have the advantage of being cheaper than traditional funds run by human managers and many investors argue that even a good manager may struggle to overcome this cost difference.

The debate about the relative merits of the two types of fund is huge in the investment world and no consensus has yet been reached. Some are vociferous in their belief in one type or the other. Others are more measured and believe that there can be a place for both, with the decision for each investor depending on factors such as investment goals, the investment time frame, the types of asset considered and how much time and effort they want to devote to choosing and managing their investments.

We are in the pragmatic camp and would be happy to include tracker funds in the portfolios if we believed that they could carry out the task expected of any of the existing actively managed funds. Currently we are not convinced that this is possible.

## Income versus accumulation units

One source of confusion for anyone who buys an investment fund for the first time is that they will be confronted with a choice between two varieties, income (inc) or accumulation (acc).

The distinction relates to what the fund does with the income it receives on its assets, such as dividends from shares, interest from bonds or rent from properties. If you buy the income version of the fund the income is paid to you at regular intervals – such as twice per year, quarterly or monthly – whereas with the accumulation type the fund manager retains the income and reinvests it.

You will therefore want the income version of the funds, as you are creating your portfolio to pay you an income. For an explanation of how to withdraw your income from your portfolio, see Chapter Five.

Our portfolios also hold some investment trusts, which will automatically pay income to you, as opposed to reinvesting it.

*Now that you understand the essential aspects of the funds within the portfolios, we will explain how we went about choosing the funds to include in the portfolios.*

---

## How did we choose these funds?

With literally thousands of investment funds to choose from, how did we choose the funds in our portfolios?

As the adverts always say, "past performance is no guide to the future". Just because a fund manager has done well in the past, it does not mean he or she will do well in future. There is luck in investing, just as in any other sphere. You do not want to choose an investment because the fund manager has simply had a recent streak of luck.

So, while we have met and interviewed the majority of fund managers who oversee the funds we recommend, we are not recommending these funds purely on the track record of the man or woman in charge.

The track record of the fund – by which we mean a lengthy history of outperforming the wider market – is only one factor.

Another vital factor is the consistency of the approach taken by the manager.

When assessing fund managers we look to identify a clear investment philosophy underpinning their approach. We also require evidence that this philosophy has been applied and followed in a consistent, disciplined way over time. While we believe that some individuals appear to have a remarkable skill for identifying attractive opportunities, we want more than that: we want evidence of a process underpinning their portfolio and the investment decisions made.

Thus it is also important that the man or woman overseeing the fund is part of a wider team, where the whole team is equally committed to the investment approach and equally committed to applying it in a way that is consistent and incorporates appropriate risk controls.

On this basis, we can expect certain fund managers' approaches to result in generally predictable performance outcomes in certain market conditions. We can expect the funds to continue to perform well even where there are changes in key personnel. This consistency of approach and execution is important for another reason: it can help us decide what funds work best when held alongside one another.

### There is no single, "right" portfolio selection

Many readers will want to make their own fund choices. You may already have your own portfolio built out of your own knowledge and experience. You may also find guidance or information provided by your chosen investment provider, pointing you towards a different selection of funds.

While here we have chosen "actively managed" funds, there are valid alternatives which track indices and therefore do not have a style or philosophy. These can be highly cost-effective and for many provide the reassurance that whatever the markets bring, at least your fund will not underperform markets by very much.

No matter how much expertise and effort go into choosing a particular fund portfolio, there is no chance that it will turn out to be the very best performer of all the potential combinations (which number in many millions). A more realistic expectation is that the portfolio will produce the income desired along with sufficient diversification to reduce the risk of alarming falls in value.

Many of the funds named in this book form part of the authors' own portfolios, even though they are not yet retired, and can be expected, assuming that nothing changes, to form a large part of their actual retirement portfolios when the time comes.

---

# Construction of the portfolios

## How we chose the mix of assets in the portfolios

The range of assets in all the portfolios includes shares, bonds (which pay interest like bank accounts but can fluctuate in value like shares) and commercial property. These three types of assets produce income in different ways, which is important because it reduces the likelihood of sharp fluctuations in the income produced by the portfolio as a whole.

Imagine, for example, that an event such as a recession affects the income you get from your shares. But the income from your bonds and from your property funds could well be unaffected. This is because the income paid by bond issuers and the tenants of commercial properties is set in stone by binding contracts, whereas dividends from shares are paid at the discretion of the firm concerned.

*Why not just stick to bonds and property then?*

The reason is that interest from bonds is reliable (as long as they are chosen carefully), but does not rise. The capital value of bonds, taken in the round, is broadly static over the long term too (although short-term fluctuations in the value of some bonds can be marked). The property market moves to its own cycles, which can involve falls in capital values. The dividends from a basket of well chosen shares, meanwhile, have the potential to rise appreciably each year.

As we said, the best approach is to hold a mixture of these assets, so that your income is not too dependent on any one of them. There is more than one way to achieve the intended mix. To simplify the argument, you could buy one fund that invests in shares, one that invests in bonds and one that invests in property. Alternatively, there are funds that hold two of these categories, or all three. We use a blend of these approaches.

## Why the portfolios seem similar

You will notice that the same funds appear in two or even all three of our portfolios. This is because what the portfolio produces – in terms of the balance between the income taken during retirement and the capital available ultimately to leave to your heirs – depends on how you handle the portfolio, not its composition.

The high-income portfolio, for example, could function very well as the inheritance (capital preservation) portfolio, if less income were taken from it.

## How will these portfolios perform?

It would be lovely to think that the portfolios will deliver exactly on the aims we have assigned to them. But markets are too unpredictable for that.

The inheritance portfolio, for example, which aims to deliver 3% annual income and preservation of your original pot of money in real terms, could end up producing a much larger sum by the time you die. With the compromise portfolio, meanwhile, you could find that taking out 4% a year, with the amount increasing every year in line with inflation, erodes the capital to some extent. It all depends on how the markets in general, and the particular investments we have chosen, perform in future.

What we can say is that if markets broadly perform in line with historic trends, the three portfolios should achieve roughly what they are intended to.

## The cash buffer

Just before we introduce the portfolios in which the great majority of your pension pot will be invested, we need to mention a vitally important subject: the need to keep a substantial sum in cash.

There are a couple of reasons to have a cash buffer. The first is that if the economy or stock market takes a very severe beating and the income paid by your funds falls, you can use the cash buffer to maintain your desired level of income. Another is to guard against any technical or administrative problems at your platform or funds that could mean a delay to the payment of your normal income.

You should set aside enough money to meet your normal income needs for one year (see page 72) and hold it in an easy-access savings account with a bank or building society.

## Calculate your income needs in retirement

In order to prepare your finances for retirement effectively, you need to know how much income you'll require after retirement.

List all items of expenditure, including all daily, weekly, monthly and annual payments. Be sure to cover the less obvious ones, such as subscriptions, membership fees, the TV licence, and even travel spending and gifts.

Then add 10% for unexpected spending. If you are some way from retirement, be sure to account for inflation (assume an inflation rate of 2.5% and use an online calculator such as the one at www.calculator.net/inflation-calculator.html).

There you have it – you now know the amount of cash to keep in your cash buffer.

# Our three income portfolios

Now that we have explained what our portfolios are intended to achieve and how we have arrived at the mix of assets, it's time to present the individual holdings. You can read more about these funds – and how and why we chose them – further on in this chapter.

If you are an experienced or confident investor, you may wish to use the following as a basic guide around which to adjust your existing portfolio. But we have designed these portfolios with the novice investor in mind: we are confident that if you invest as outlined here you will be in an excellent position to meet your goals.

Select one of the three portfolios below that suits you best. You then log in to the account where your amalgamated pension is held and invest your pot in the funds in the percentages shown, ensuring of course that your one-year cash buffer is intact.

For now, we just show the composition of the portfolios – the funds that they hold. For an explanation of how to actually take income from the portfolios, see Chapter Five.

## Portfolio 1: The high-income portfolio

Target: an annual income of 5% of the initial portfolio value. We want this income to rise each year roughly in line with inflation – if, for example, you have put £100,000 into the portfolio and therefore expect an income of £5,000 in the first year, inflation of 2% would increase the target income to £5,100 the following year. There is an acceptance that the capital is likely to be eroded over time.

With this portfolio, but not the others, the expectation is that you will need to buy an annuity at some stage. This is because with this portfolio you will make small sales from your fund holdings regularly to top up the natural income. Eventually, this approach involves the purchase of an annuity, to avoid reaching a point where erosion of capital leads to a steep decline in the natural income and hence a need to sell even more assets to maintain the target income – a process that might eventually exhaust your pension pot.

### Cash reserve

• One year's worth of target income held outside the pension in an easy-access savings account or cash ISA.

### Four stock market funds

• Artemis Income fund (12.5% of the portfolio)

• Ardevora UK Income fund (12.5% of the portfolio)

• Montanaro UK Income fund (12.5% of the portfolio)

• LF Miton UK Multi Cap Income fund (12.5% of the portfolio)

### Two funds that invest in bonds

• Janus Henderson Strategic Bond (12.5% of the portfolio)

• Jupiter Strategic Bond (12.5% of the portfolio)

### Two funds that invest in commercial property

• Standard Life Investments Property Income (12.5% of the portfolio)

• Regional REIT (real estate investment trust) (12.5% of the portfolio)

Starting with a pension pot of £300,000, the table below shows the **high-income portfolio**.

| Fund | Type | Share class | Amount invested | Yield | Annual income | Dividend frequency | 1st div of year | SEDOL code* | ISIN code* |
|---|---|---|---|---|---|---|---|---|---|
| Artemis Income | Fund | I £ Income | £37,500 | 4.48% | £1,680 | Half-yrly | 30 Jun | B2PLJJ3 | GB00B2PLJJ36 |
| Ardevora UK Income | Fund | C £ Income | £37,500 | 4.40% | £1,650 | Half-yrly | End Feb | B4XXXL5 | IE00B4XXXL53 |
| Montanaro UK Income | Fund | £ unhedged | £37,500 | 3.61% | £1,354 | Qtly | Start Jan | B1FZRT4 | IE00B1FZRT49 |
| LF Miton UK Multi Cap Income | Fund | B income | £37,500 | 4.58% | £1,718 | Qtly | End Jan | B4M24M1 | GB00B4M24M14 |
| Janus Henderson Strategic Bond | Fund | I income | £37,500 | 3.39% | £1,271 | Qtly | End Feb | 750208 | GB0007502080 |
| Jupiter Strategic Bond | Fund | I income | £37,500 | 3.88% | £1,455 | Qtly | Late Mar | B544HM3 | GB00B544HM32 |
| Standard Life Inv Property Income | Inv trust | N/A | £37,500 | 5.55% | £2,081 | Qtly | Late Mar | 3387528 | GB0033875286 |
| Regional REIT | Inv trust | N/A | £37,500 | 8.68% | £3,244 | Qtly | Mid Apr | BYV2ZQ3 | GG00BYV2ZQ34 |
| Total/average | | | £300,000 | 4.82% | £14,453 | | | | |

*These SEDOL and ISIN numbers are correct for Interactive Investor and several others. However, some platforms (e.g., Hargreaves Lansdown) negotiate special deals on fund charges that necessitate different SEDOL and ISIN numbers. In this case check the fund name, annual charge and type (choose income as opposed to accumulation) carefully.

## Portfolio 2: The inheritance portfolio

Target: an annual income of 3% of the initial portfolio value, rising with inflation, with maintained or increasing capital value in real terms, so that a large legacy can be left. Only natural income will be taken, so your capital will not be eroded by withdrawals and there should be no need to buy an annuity at any stage.

### Cash reserve

• One year's worth of target income held outside the pension in an easy-access savings account.

### One mixed-asset fund

• Troy Trojan fund (12.5% of the portfolio)

### Two income-focused investment trusts

• City of London (12.5% of the portfolio)

• Temple Bar (12.5% of the portfolio)

### One global stock market fund that targets growth

• Fundsmith Equity fund (12.5% of the portfolio)

### Two funds that invest in bonds

• Janus Henderson Strategic Bond (12.5% of the portfolio)

• Jupiter Strategic Bond (12.5% of the portfolio)

### Two funds that invest in commercial property

• Standard Life Investments Property Income (12.5% of the portfolio)

• Regional REIT (real estate investment trust) (12.5% of the portfolio)

Starting with a pension pot of £300,000, the table below shows the **inheritance portfolio**.

| Fund | Type | Share class | Yield | Amount invested | Annual income | Dividend frequency | 1st div of year | SEDOL code* | ISIN code* |
|---|---|---|---|---|---|---|---|---|---|
| Fundsmith Equity | Fund | I income | 0.69% | £37,500 | £259 | Half-yrly | End Feb | B4MR8G8 | GB00B4MR8G82 |
| Troy Trojan | Fund | O income | 0.50% | £37,500 | £188 | Half-yrly | End Mar | 3424373 | GB0034243732 |
| City of London | Inv trust | N/A | 4.52% | £37,500 | £1,695 | Qtly | End Feb | 199049 | GB0001990497 |
| Temple Bar | Inv trust | N/A | 3.60% | £37,500 | £1,350 | Qtly | End Mar | 882532 | GB0008825324 |
| Janus Henderson Strategic Bond | Fund | I income | 3.39% | £37,500 | £1,271 | Qtly | End Feb | 750208 | GB0007502080 |
| Jupiter Strategic Bond | Fund | I income | 3.88% | £37,500 | £1,455 | Qtly | Late Mar | B544HM3 | GB00B544HM32 |
| Standard Life Inv Property Income | Inv trust | N/A | 5.55% | £37,500 | £2,081 | Qtly | Late Mar | 3387528 | GB0033875286 |
| Regional REIT | Inv trust | N/A | 8.65% | £37,500 | £3,244 | Qtly | Mid Apr | BYV2ZQ3 | GG00BYV2ZQ34 |
| **Total/average** | | | **3.85%** | **£300,000** | **£11,543** | | | | |

*These SEDOL and ISIN numbers are correct for Interactive Investor and several others. However, some platforms (e.g., Hargreaves Lansdown) negotiate special deals on fund charges that necessitate different SEDOL and ISIN numbers. In this case check the fund name, annual charge and type (choose income as opposed to accumulation) carefully.

## Portfolio 3: The compromise portfolio

Target: an annual income of 4% of the initial portfolio value, rising each year roughly in line with inflation, with little or no erosion of capital, so that an appreciable legacy can be left. It may be necessary to buy an annuity at some stage, but if so the intention is that only part of your pot will be used for this – leaving cash behind that can be left to your heirs. No regular sale of part of your holdings to top up the natural income is intended.

### Cash reserve

- One year's worth of target income held outside the pension in an easy-access savings account.

### Four UK-focused stock market funds

- Artemis Income fund (12.5% of the portfolio)

- Ardevora UK Income fund (12.5% of the portfolio)

- Montanaro UK Income fund (12.5% of the portfolio)

- LF Miton UK Multi Cap Income fund (12.5% of the portfolio)

### Two funds that invest in bonds

- Janus Henderson Strategic Bond fund (12.5% of the portfolio)

- Jupiter Strategic Bond fund (12.5% of the portfolio)

### Two funds that invest in commercial property

- Standard Life Investments Property Income (12.5% of the portfolio)

- Regional REIT (real estate investment trust) (12.5% of the portfolio)

Starting with a pension pot of £300,000, the table below shows the **compromise portfolio**.

| Fund | Type | Share class | Amount invested | Yield | Annual income | Dividend frequency | 1st div of year | SEDOL code* | ISIN code* |
|---|---|---|---|---|---|---|---|---|---|
| Artemis Income | Fund | I Income | £37,500 | 4.48% | £1,680 | Half-yrly | 30 Jun | B2PLJJ3 | GB00B2PLJJ36 |
| Ardevora UK Income | Fund | C £ Income | £37,500 | 4.40% | £1,650 | Half-yrly | End Feb | B4XXXL5 | IE00B4XXXL53 |
| Montanaro UK Income | Fund | £ unhedged | £37,500 | 3.61% | £1,354 | Qtly | Start Jan | B1FZRT4 | IE00B1FZRT49 |
| LF Miton UK Multi Cap Income | Fund | B income | £37,500 | 4.58% | £1,718 | Qtly | End Jan | B4M24M1 | GB00B4M24M14 |
| Janus Henderson Strategic Bond | Fund | I income | £37,500 | 3.39% | £1,271 | Qtly | End Feb | 750208 | GB0007502080 |
| Jupiter Strategic Bond | Fund | I income | £37,500 | 3.88% | £1,455 | Qtly | Late Mar | B544HM3 | GB00B544HM32 |
| Standard Life Inv Property Income | Inv trust | N/A | £37,500 | 5.55% | £2,081 | Qtly | Late Mar | 3387528 | GB0033875286 |
| Regional REIT | Inv trust | N/A | £37,500 | 8.65% | £3,244 | Qtly | Mid Apr | BYV2ZQ3 | GG00BYV2ZQ34 |
| **Total/average** | | | **£300,000** | **4.82%** | **£14,453** | | | | |

*These SEDOL and ISIN numbers are correct for Interactive Investor and several others. However, some platforms (e.g., Hargreaves Lansdown) negotiate special deals on fund charges that necessitate different SEDOL and ISIN numbers. In this case check the fund name, annual charge and type (choose income as opposed to accumulation) carefully.

# Why we chose these particular funds

When selecting the funds to include in our portfolios, we looked for long and stable performance track records and experienced managers who were able to explain their strategies clearly. In many cases, we have met the managers and had the opportunity to question them at length about their investment philosophy.

## Artemis Income

**Artemis Income** has been managed since 2002 by one of Britain's most experienced income investors, Adrian Frost, in conjunction with Nick Shenton and Andy Marsh, who joined more recently. The fund is therefore well prepared for Mr Frost's eventual retirement, although there is no reason to expect it to be imminent. He was one of the first fund managers to be alert to the threat posed to incumbent companies by new, disruptive digital businesses.

**How to ensure you buy these exact fund:** look for the exact fund name on your investment platform. Or check the SEDOL or ISIN number, shown in the table. Buy the *income* units, not accumulation units.

## Ardevora UK Income

This fund is managed by Jeremy Lang and William Pattisson, who over long careers have developed a unique style of investing. They analyse companies' financial position in depth, but also consider psychological biases on the part of company managers and investors that can result in shares being too cheaply (or too expensively) valued. The fund has outperformed its peer group since its launch.

**How to ensure you buy this exact fund:** look for this exact name on your investment platform (the name may be prefixed by Margetts or MGTS). Or check the SEDOL or ISIN number, shown in the table. Buy the *income* units.

## Montanaro UK Income

Another fund run by an experienced manager, in this case Charles Montanaro. He founded the management company in 1991. He holds, indirectly, a large stake in the fund, so his interests are well aligned with those of ordinary investors.

**How to ensure you buy this exact fund:** look for this exact name on your investment platform. Or check the SEDOL or ISIN number, shown in the table. Buy the *income* units.

## Miton UK Multi Cap Income

This fund, which invests in British companies of all sizes, is managed by the respected team of Gervais Williams and Martin Turner, who have almost 60 years of industry experience between them. By holding stakes in a large number of companies (150 at the time of writing) the fund aims to control risk. This is borne out by the fund coming third out of almost 100 funds in its sector when ranked according to one indicator of steady returns. Performance has been strong too, with that same third-place position for total returns (including dividends) over five years.

**How to ensure you buy this exact fund:** look for this exact name on your investment platform. It may be preceded by "LF". Or check the SEDOL or ISIN number, shown in the table. Buy the *income* units.

## City of London Investment Trust

The **City of London Investment Trust** has an extraordinary record: founded in 1891, it has increased its dividend in every one of the past 52 years. It is conservatively managed, with holdings in many of Britain's largest companies. It should therefore continue to provide a reliable income for holders of our portfolios for many years to come. As an investment trust it is well suited to the inheritance portfolio: it would cost you money in fees from your platform if you sold a small part of the holding each quarter to contribute to your income, but such asset sales are not necessary in the inheritance portfolio.

**How to ensure you buy this exact fund:** look for the stock market ticker symbol CTY. Or check the SEDOL or ISIN number, shown in the table.

## Temple Bar Investment Trust

The manager of this trust, Alastair Mundy, takes a "contrarian" approach to income investing, which means buying shares in companies that are out of favour with the wider market in the belief that they will in time recover. The fund has outperformed the stock market as a whole over the past five years. This is another investment trust, so we have chosen it for the inheritance portfolio.

**How to ensure you buy this exact fund:** look for the stock market ticker symbol TMPL. Or check the SEDOL or ISIN number, shown in the table.

## Henderson and Jupiter Strategic Bond funds

*Strategic* bond funds achieve maximum diversification by having the ability to buy bonds of any type. Conversely, some bond funds are much more restricted; for example, there are funds that invest only in bonds issued by the British government.

The **Henderson Strategic Bond fund** is managed by the experienced team of John Pattullo and Jenna Barnard. The **Jupiter Strategic Bond fund** also has a respected and experienced manager in Ariel Bezalel.

**How to ensure you buy these exact funds:** look for these exact fund names and choose the income units. Both funds should have a share class of I, although share classes can vary between fund platforms. Or check the SEDOL or ISIN number, shown in the table. Buy the *income* units.

## Fundsmith Equity fund

The **Fundsmith Equity fund** is managed by Terry Smith, an outspoken critic of the practices of many traditional approaches to investment. He showed his ability as a stock picker before the launch of his fund when he managed the pension fund of the company he used to run, Tullett Prebon.

**How to ensure you buy this exact fund:** look for share class I – income units. Or check the SEDOL or ISIN number, shown in the table.

## Troy Trojan fund

Troy Asset Management was established to manage the money of Lord Weinstock, the former boss of GEC. The Trojan fund, run by Sebastian Lyon, has a strong bias towards avoiding losses (as opposed to chasing the biggest gains), but has still significantly outperformed the FTSE 100 index since its launch in 2001.

**How to ensure you buy this exact fund:** look for share class O – income units. Or check the SEDOL or ISIN number, shown in the table.

## Commercial Property investment trusts

The **Standard Life Investments Property Income investment trust** has high exposure to industrial property, which is expected to perform better than retail property for the foreseeable future.

**Regional REIT** (real estate investment trust) has been chosen for its minimal exposure to the London market or retail developments, investing instead largely in offices and warehouses outside the capital.

**How to ensure you buy these exact funds:** look for the stock market ticker symbols SLI (Standard Life) and RGL (Regional REIT). Or check the SEDOL or ISIN numbers, shown in the table.

Note: sometimes funds discourage new investors by imposing extra charges, perhaps 5%, when you invest for the first time. This is done because the manager does not want the fund to get bigger, which in some cases can make it harder to manage. None of the funds named above suffered from such restrictions or extra costs at the time of writing, but they could be imposed at any time. You should check, via your investment platform, before committing money. Investment trusts do not suffer from this problem.

*Now let's move ahead to Chapter Five, where we show how to withdraw the income from your portfolio and manage the portfolio over time.*

## Chapter Five
# Taking Sustainable Income from Your Portfolio

**"How do I take the right amount of income from my portfolio?"**

Putting your retirement savings into a portfolio of income-producing investments is not the end of the story. You'll also need to go about taking income from your portfolio in the right way.

In addition, you'll need a rule that stops you taking too much income, which could lead to your money running out too soon. In this chapter, we introduce a simple rule to keep your income sustainable.

## Withdrawing income and monitoring your portfolio

You now have all your pension savings invested in a portfolio of funds that will, we hope, be appropriate to your needs. Even with no further action on your part, they will start to produce an income. You also have your cash buffer.

However, there are some subtleties to deal with. First, there are normally costs involved in withdrawing money from a SIPP, and these costs can be minimised with careful planning. Second, some (those who chose the high-income portfolio and possibly, in some circumstances, those who selected the compromise portfolio) will spend some of their capital as well as withdraw the income that their investments produce automatically. This deliberate spending of capital gives rise to a tricky balancing act between taking too much money and too little.

*We'll now cover these two issues in turn.*

# How to withdraw income from your pension

Taking money from your pension is not quite the same as withdrawing it from a bank account. First you need to determine whether the amount you want to withdraw can be met by the income that has been produced naturally by your investments, or whether you'll need to sell a small slice of your assets too (see the following box for an explanation of natural income in the context of our portfolios).

---

## The natural income of our portfolios

When you have invested your pension in one of the portfolios in the previous chapter, there are two ways in which you can take an income from it. This topic was introduced in Chapter Three, but here we cover it in more detail.

The first is simply to take the income that your funds produce automatically. Our stock market funds, for instance, produce dividends, typically paid quarterly. As we have chosen the income as opposed to accumulation fund variants, these dividends will be paid as a matter of course into the cash account of your SIPP. Investment trusts also pay income straight to your SIPP in the same way. You can then withdraw this cash when you like – we refer to this as *taking the natural income*.

The natural income produced by our high-income portfolio is about 4%. To achieve the target of a total income of 5% of the initial portfolio value, that natural income needs to be supplemented by regular sales of the assets themselves, amounting to about 1% of the portfolio each year.

While the natural income is paid into your cash account automatically, you need to take action to get the extra money from asset sales. You'll need to go into your account and sell the appropriate number of shares or fund units to produce the extra income. As explained in the main text, we will aim to sell a fixed number of shares or fund units, rather than aiming to raise a particular sum, as this method is better for the long-term sustainability of your income.

---

Then come the mechanics of the withdrawals. As said, the income produced naturally by your investments will be paid automatically into the cash account that comes with your SIPP and can be withdrawn from there at the click of a mouse. But if that income was not enough to cover your intended withdrawal and you need to make a partial sale of assets as well, you will often be charged a fee for doing this. All platforms charge for selling shares in investment trusts, while some charge when you sell ordinary funds too. On top of this there is sometimes a charge for taking money out of the pension, even if it is held in cash within the pension.

Because of these charges, withdraw money only four times a year, rather than monthly. At each withdrawal, take out enough cash to last you for the next three months.

Most of the funds we have chosen for our portfolios pay dividends quarterly, which will suit this schedule nicely, although one or two pay at six-monthly or monthly intervals.

There are likely to be times when the amount you expect to withdraw from naturally generated income (that is, before selling any assets) has not actually arrived in your SIPP cash account because the payment date for one or more dividends has not yet arrived. For this reason, we suggest keeping a small balance in this account, say a month's worth of income, so that you can withdraw the amount you need when you want it, knowing that the account will be replenished before long when the dividend is received. If for some reason there is still not enough in the SIPP cash account to meet your income needs for that quarter, you can draw money from your main cash buffer, replenishing it when possible.

## The biggest danger to your pension savings – and how to deal with it

Now we come to the other important aspect of withdrawing money from your pension: the need to ensure that your income is not excessive, which could cause irreversible damage and derail the vital requirement to provide an income for the rest of your life.

If the financial markets could be relied on to rise smoothly at their average historic pace, there would be no problem: you could sit back and simply spend the income as it was produced – and, if need be, gradually sell assets at regular intervals to boost your income.

As we all know, the markets cannot be relied on to behave in this convenient way. This can pose acute dangers for anyone who relies on a portfolio of investments for retirement income.

This warning applies to anyone who tops up the natural income of their portfolio with periodic sales of assets – so it will definitely apply to those who have invested their money in the high-income portfolio and could also affect those who opt for the compromise portfolio; we cannot say for sure as it will depend on the yield of this portfolio at the time you invest, which varies constantly.

However, the warning does not apply to those who take only the natural income, in other words those who have invested in the inheritance portfolio and perhaps, depending on the yield at the time, those who invested in the compromise portfolio.

Let's imagine that you have £300,000 in your pension and that it is invested in the high-income portfolio, which is intended to generate 5% income a year. Your target income from the portfolio is therefore

£15,000 a year, equal to £1,250 a month or £3,750 a quarter (this target income will increase every year in line with inflation).

The natural yield of the high-income portfolio at the time of writing is 4.24% (we will aim to publish up-to-date figures on our website, www.pensionincomeinvestor.com), which equates to £12,709 a year, £1,059 a month, or £3,177 a quarter. This means that the natural yield falls short of your quarterly income target of £3,750 by about £573 a quarter (or £2,291 a year).

You raise the extra money you need by selling a small proportion of your total pension assets every quarter.

We suspect that this idea causes disquiet among some savers, who feel that by eroding their capital, even slightly, they are on a slippery slope that will end in them having nothing. But in fact selling assets slowly can make perfect sense.

If you refuse to use any of your capital, you guarantee that there will be something left unspent when you die. Of course, some people want this, and the inheritance and compromise portfolios are designed for them. But those with more modest savings will normally need to take as much income from their pension as possible for their own needs, and that means not leaving money behind for the next generation.

Look at the question of gradually selling assets another way. At the age of 75, you will clearly need less money to fund the remainder of your retirement than you did at 65, so why not spend the difference in that time?

However, for anyone who does gradually sell assets as opposed to relying on the income generated naturally, there is an important caveat.

Over the course of a normal retirement there are bound to be times when the stock market falls significantly. For example, the FTSE 100 index of Britain's biggest companies has fallen by 20% or more on five occasions in the past 30 years (in 1987, 1998, 2000–03, 2007–09 and 2015–16). On this basis, we can expect on average a fall of this severity every six years.

If you are used to selling, to use the example above, £573-worth of your assets every quarter to top up the natural income, you will have to sell more shares (or fund units) to raise that sum if the markets have just fallen.

For example, let's simplify matters and assume that you have just one fund and its unit price has just fallen from 100p to 90p. At 100p you would need to sell 573 units to generate the £573 you want, but if the units are worth just 90p each you will need to sell 636.5 of them to get the same sum.

But selling more units than you expected also means that, when you come to make your next withdrawal, you have fewer units left generating natural income. As a result, your future income requirements will in turn have to be met by more sales. These sales again diminish the number of units left. In this way, a vicious cycle can be established that could see your capital eroded much more quickly than you had intended.

Fortunately, there is an easy way to avoid being caught by this trap.

## Your exact tactics for selling assets to boost your income

Selling too many assets when they have fallen in value puts the long-term sustainability of your income at risk, as we have just explained.

There is also a related danger: being tempted to sell more of your assets when they have gone up in value. You might say to yourself: "Oh look, my pot has risen by 10% – why don't I take that extra money and spend it?"

In fact this would be a dangerous course of action: selling 10% of your assets means that they would produce 10% less natural income in future – a shortfall that you would have to make up by selling even more assets from that point onwards, starting the same vicious circle we warned about above.

To avoid both of these dangers, we have this simple rule to keep your income sustainable: *sell a maximum of 1% of your original fund units or shares each year (0.25% a quarter).*

Note that you are not selling 0.25% of the value of the fund at the time, but 0.25% of the number of fund units or shares that you bought when you set up your portfolio at the outset. You will therefore need to keep handy a record of this information.

Using this rule means that the ability of your overall pot to generate natural income will decline by 1% a year, which is manageable; a 10% decline, for example, would not be!

How you spread asset sales across the various funds in your portfolio also matters. Our rule is to sell a maximum of 0.25% of the units (or shares) *in each fund* every quarter, irrespective of whether each fund has risen or fallen in value.

This, apart from being simpler than other possible approaches, preserves the income-producing potential of each fund and avoids having to take a bet on which ones are likely to perform better in the future. It also means that you are preserving the overall portfolio's original division of income-generating potential between the various types of asset (shares, bonds and property).

If the value of the portfolio as a whole has gone up, the amount you realise from selling 0.25% of it will also increase, so your available income *does* rise. You may choose to take less than 0.25% of course, which would be good for the long-term health of the fund. Or you may, if you have previously had to dip into the main cash reserve, top it up again with the extra money.

*If, however, the overall value has fallen, you should still limit asset sales to 0.25% a quarter, making up any shortfall in your income from your main cash reserve.*

The following table shows how this process might work for one fund, with £37,500 invested in it at the outset. We have imagined that the fund price rises slightly in the first year, falls in the second and then recovers. The income, by contrast, rises more steadily from one year to the next.

Table 5.1: The process for selling assets to boost your income

| Year | Quarter | Number of units held | Value per unit on day of withdrawal | Value of your holding of the fund on day of withdrawal | Dividend per unit (p) | Natural income (dividend per unit x number of units) | Number of units to be sold | Amount raised by selling 0.25% of original fund units | Total income (natural income + amount raised by sale) | Total withdrawal as percentage of original amount invested | Remaining fund value |
|---|---|---|---|---|---|---|---|---|---|---|---|
| 2020 | 1 | 37500.0 | £1.00 | £37,500 | 0.0100 | £375.00 | 93.75 | £93.75 | £468.75 | | £37,406.25 |
| 2020 | 2 | 37406.3 | £1.01 | £37,780 | 0.0100 | £374.06 | 93.75 | £94.69 | £468.75 | | £37,685.63 |
| 2020 | 3 | 37312.5 | £1.02 | £38,059 | 0.0100 | £373.13 | 93.75 | £95.63 | £468.75 | | £37,963.13 |
| 2020 | 4 | 37218.8 | £1.04 | £38,708 | 0.0100 | £372.19 | 93.75 | £97.50 | £469.69 | | £38,610.00 |
| Total for year | | | | | 0.0400 | £1,494.38 | 375 | £381.56 | £1,875.94 | 5.00% | |
| 2021 | 1 | 37125.0 | £1.02 | £38,250 | 0.0105 | £389.81 | 93.75 | £95.63 | £485.44 | | £37,771.88 |
| 2021 | 2 | 37031.3 | £0.99 | £37,125 | 0.0105 | £388.83 | 93.75 | £92.81 | £481.64 | | £36,568.13 |
| 2021 | 3 | 36937.5 | £0.98 | £36,750 | 0.0105 | £387.84 | 93.75 | £91.88 | £479.72 | | £36,106.88 |
| 2021 | 4 | 36843.8 | £0.96 | £36,000 | 0.0105 | £386.86 | 93.75 | £90.00 | £476.86 | | £35,280.00 |
| Total for year | | | | | 0.0420 | £1,553.34 | 375 | £370.31 | £1,923.66 | 5.13% | |

| Year | Quarter | Number of units held | Value per unit on day of withdrawal | Value of your holding of the fund on day of withdrawal | Dividend per unit (p) | Natural income (dividend per unit x number of units) | Number of units to be sold | Amount raised by selling 0.25% of original fund units | Total income (natural income + amount raised by sale) | Total withdrawal as percentage of original amount invested | Remaining fund value |
|---|---|---|---|---|---|---|---|---|---|---|---|
| 2022 | 1 | 36750.0 | £1.00 | £37,500 | 0.0110 | £404.25 | 93.75 | £93.75 | £498.00 | | £36,656.25 |
| 2022 | 2 | 36656.3 | £1.02 | £38,250 | 0.0110 | £403.22 | 93.75 | £95.63 | £498.84 | | £37,293.75 |
| 2022 | 3 | 36562.5 | £1.04 | £39,000 | 0.0110 | £402.19 | 93.75 | £97.50 | £499.69 | | £37,927.50 |
| 2022 | 4 | 36468.8 | £1.06 | £39,750 | 0.0110 | £401.16 | 93.75 | £99.38 | £500.53 | | £38,557.50 |
| Total for year | | | | | 0.0440 | £1,610.81 | 375 | £386.25 | £1,997.06 | 5.33% | |

There are several things to note about the table:

- We have made some fairly benign assumptions about how the fund price fluctuates. If the markets were to hit a bad patch the price could fall more severely. Our practice of selling a set number of units each quarter, as opposed to selling enough units to raise a particular sum, prevents excessive erosion of capital. If this causes too large an income shortfall, the difference should be made up from the main cash reserve.

- In the second year we have assumed that the dividend has risen even while the fund price has fallen. This is perfectly possible, because the two things are subject to different dynamics. The dividend depends on the underlying performance and profitability of the businesses that the fund invests in, whereas the price reflects the subjective, often short-term opinions and sentiments of the stock market. It is not unreasonable to hope that dividend rises over time will tend to outweigh any loss of income caused by falls in fund prices, although there can be no guarantee.

- Under our benign assumptions, the holding in the fund is worth more after three years than at the outset, even though some units have been sold. Again, this cannot be guaranteed. Our approach is deliberately conservative and designed to cope with more extreme market gyrations, which could result in the holding being worth substantially less after three or more years. As long as the fall is not extreme, this is in line with our strategy and not likely to be a problem.

- The total income from the natural yield and the sales of units rises, under our assumptions, from one year to the next. Again, this cannot be guaranteed.

- A fractional number of units is sold each quarter. This is no problem for ordinary funds, such as Artemis Income, but sales of shares in investment trusts, such as City of London, have to be made in whole numbers. You may have to make slight adjustments from quarter to quarter to accommodate this.

## Example

*"I have an investment portfolio that produces an income for me and my husband, but for the past six months the natural income from the portfolio has dropped and is not sufficient for us to live on. How do I top up this income through other means?"*

This is the kind of situation that many retired people could face, although we hope that the portfolios we have suggested will minimise the risk of such an outcome.

If it does happen, the first thing to ask is whether the fall in natural income is likely to be temporary or permanent. If temporary, the ideal source of top-up income would be your cash buffer. If permanent, on the other hand, and you had to use the cash buffer indefinitely, it would eventually run dry.

If you had been relying on the natural income alone up to this point, it would be fine to make some asset sales in addition, although not beyond our suggested level of 1% a year.

If you had already been selling 1% of your assets a year (and expect the decline in natural income to be permanent), it could be worth getting some annuity quotes. Depending on your age and state of health (and your husband's), you could find that your remaining pension pot would buy the annual income you need. You would need to specify a *joint-life* annuity as you are a couple. An annuity with annual increases, whether these are in line with inflation or by a fixed amount each year, would be a good idea.

If none of those suggestions works, you may need to consider releasing some of the money tied up in the value of your home and using it to top up your investment portfolio, thereby generating more income (see Chapter Ten for more on taking money from your property).

## When do I need to consider changing the investments in my portfolio?

If you invest your retirement pot in the portfolios we have suggested, or any similar basket of investments, you'll need to keep a close eye on the funds involved.

There are two main things to watch out for.

First, a change in fund manager. We have chosen the funds in our portfolios partly because of the reputation and record of the individuals in charge. When these people retire or move on, investors at the very least need to consider whether to switch to an alternative fund.

When fund managers leave, fund management firms tend to put out statements along the lines of, "we have a strong team in place and our process will remain unchanged". Treat these statements with a degree of scepticism. Form your own opinion – perhaps with help from the personal finance sections of national newspapers or from specialist websites such as www.morningstar.co.uk or www.citywire. co.uk – of the merits of the new managers relative to the alternative funds available. We intend to keep up-to-date information on the best alternatives on our website, www.pensionincomeinvestor.com.

The other important task is to monitor performance. This is not a question of looking every day at the ups and downs of the price of our funds, but a matter of spotting any consistent failure to perform in line with similar funds over a period of two or three years. There are tools that allow you to compare a fund's performance with its peers on platforms (Hargreaves Lansdown has one, which both customers and non-customers can use) and we will aim to keep track of the funds in our portfolios on our website.

There are other circumstances in which you may want to change the portfolio. This has nothing to do with individual funds, but concerns the types of asset that you hold. There is an argument that investors should switch to less volatile assets, principally bonds, as they approach the point at which they want to buy an annuity, as we expect investors in the high-income portfolio to need to do at some stage. We believe that such a switch to bonds is a sensible course of action in general, although the situation at the time of writing is complicated by the fact that the safest bonds are widely seen as overvalued and highly priced. We cannot say at this stage what the best course of action will be in, say, ten years' time.

---

## How much time should you spend looking over your portfolio and measuring its performance?

**Mark Dampier** has run the fund research team at Hargreaves Lansdown, Britain's biggest investment platform, for many years and is an experienced private investor.

★ ★ ★

Personally, I don't spend a lot of time analysing the performance of my portfolio in great detail. That is partly because I live with the business every day of the week. Another factor is that, with a relatively mature pot of savings, I am now pretty well diversified and I am not expecting spectacular gains from one year to the next.

My primary aim is to generate future income, not to shoot the lights out with capital appreciation, happy though I am to take it when it occurs. I am getting more risk-averse as I get older.

Many investment websites have tools that enable you to drill down through your holdings to analyse what you own – and how well you have done – in huge detail. I certainly wouldn't want to stop you doing that once in a while, but I question how much value you will get in return for the time it takes. The danger is that you end up with so much information that it paralyses you, stopping you from making any decisions.

Provided that I am broadly happy with the overall mix of my portfolio, I prefer to focus on the funds that I already own. If they are doing what they promised to do, I can't see an urgent need to change anything, unless they have become a disproportionately large part of what I have. Of course there are always tempting new opportunities to consider, but I simply caution that if you are happy with what you have, you don't need to be rushed into action.

My own bias has always been to stick with funds where the manager has a huge amount of experience and a proven track record over more than one economic and market cycle. I rarely invest in funds whose manager has less than a ten-year performance record for that reason (although that track record could have begun at another firm).

It is rare for me to sell funds that I have held for a long time. Once you have decided that you have found a manager of real and rare talent, it makes no sense to jettison them without good reason. My holding period for funds typically runs to several years.

When I do sell, it is as often as not because I have other portfolio considerations in mind, not because I have changed my mind about the quality of the fund or the talent of its manager. That said, there are occasions – for example, when a manager moves company or simply retires – when you have to say goodbye to an old favourite.

*This is an edited extract from Mark Dampier's book* Effective Investing, *published by Harriman House.*

# Chapter Six
# The End Game: How to Maintain Your Income in the Later Years

**"What happens in the later stages of retirement?"**

In Chapter Five we covered how to maximise retirement income from a fixed pot of money by augmenting the natural income with withdrawals from capital.

This chapter deals with the problems that arise 20 or 30 years into retirement, where you are not likely to want uncertainty around your income and remaining capital.

## The need to buy an annuity later in life

As you take an income, you can expect the amount of money left in your pension pot to decline each year. This makes sense, because as you get older the total amount of capital needed for your remaining lifespan is less. (Remember though that our inheritance portfolio is designed not to decline in value each year, because just the natural income is taken from it, leaving the capital untouched and able to grow. If you intend to invest in this portfolio, you need not read this chapter.)

If you knew exactly how long you would live, this method would work perfectly right to the end. Unfortunately, longevity is unknown, so the method breaks down as we age – living even one year longer than expected would mean a year with no income from your once-large pension pot.

And, once you have started on the path of gradually spending your capital, you cannot revert to limiting withdrawals to the natural yield without seeing your income fall significantly. Taking a 4% income from a reduced pot of £400,000, for example, is not the same as taking a 4% income from a pot that began at £500,000!

*The solution? We come back to the annuity.*

We have always believed that annuities did not become completely redundant as a result of the collapse in the rates they pay and the new pension freedoms introduced in 2015. What is clear is that annuities ceased to be a viable way for most people to transform a lifetime of savings into an income for life *at the point of retirement at 65.*

But annuity rates improve as you age, as Table 6.1 shows.

**Table 6.1: How annuities become more appealing with age: for every £100,000 you spend on an annuity, this is the starting income you'll receive each year**

| Age | Starting income on £100,000 annuity |
|-----|-------------------------------------|
| 65  | £3,214 |
| 70  | £3,806 |
| 75  | £4,634 |
| 78  | £5,361 |
| 80  | £6,015 |
| 82  | £6,776 |
| 85  | £8,312 |
| 87  | £9,227 |
| 90  | £12,450 |

Notes: Annuity income guaranteed to rise by 3% per year. Your spouse will get 50% of the income if you die first. Source: Legal & General.

This means that, by your late 70s, you should be able to get an annuity that replaces the target income from the portfolio – provided that your pot has not been depleted excessively.

The 1% annual limit on capital withdrawals introduced in Chapter Five was designed with this aim in mind, with a margin of safety added. If your pot simply maintains its value – which means that its value grows by 1% a year, cancelling out the asset sales (and it's not unreasonable, based on historic trends, to expect much better growth than that) – then at age 80, say, you will be able to lock into a guaranteed income for life that is better than you would have received had you bought an annuity at the point of retirement.

Those who have the compromise portfolio and intend to leave a legacy will use only part of their pot to buy an annuity, spending enough on it to produce their target income. There will, if all has gone to plan, be enough left over after the annuity purchase to leave something to your heirs. This money can remain invested as before or, if you wish, it can be switched to the inheritance portfolio.

There is another benefit from buying an annuity at some stage: it avoids the danger of *oversaving*, by which we mean the failure to spend all of the retirement pot on its intended purpose of providing a comfortable life in retirement. This could easily be a danger if your investments perform well, but where you are understandably cautious about increasing your pension withdrawals halfway through your retirement for fear of going too far in the other direction. Buying an annuity cuts through all these conflicting considerations and simply uses all of your remaining capital (or the proportion of it that you choose to allocate to the purpose) to provide an income for the rest of your life.

Finally, getting your income from an annuity involves no effort or maintenance, so it is ideal for the later stages of retirement, when you may not have the energy, health or inclination to monitor a portfolio of investments.

If you are worried about how your spouse or partner might manage dealing with finances after your death, an annuity again provides a solution in that it would require no management on his or her part.

## A price for security

*"I spent £80,000 on an annuity to pay my service charges and electricity bills."*

Among the correspondence received by the *Telegraph's* Money Desk are those letters from readers who want to share the solutions they have found to certain problems.

One man, aged 76, with a wife of similar age, described how he managed most of their joint savings and investments to provide an income. This income was adequate but was somewhat variable; some years he was able to generate more income than others from his investments, while some years he earned less – for all the reasons covered in earlier chapters.

To reduce risk and make the general management of household bills easier, he spent £80,000 buying an annuity that would pay out for the duration of both his own and his wife's lives. The payouts would rise at 3% per year, which is more than the Bank of England's target rate of inflation of 2%.

He said:

> "We live in a small flat where we do not have a mortgage but where the service charges are about £2,000 per year. We have no gas and our electricity bills are around £900 a year. The annuity means these things are fully covered and I have the security of knowing they will be covered for my wife when I die."

At the time of writing, if you spent £80,000 on an annuity attached to the lives of a couple each aged 76, and rising at 3% per year, your payouts would start at £3,025 per year. That may not seem much – but there's a price for security, and this man was clearly happy to pay it.

## People are taking lump sums well before retirement and buying annuities well after it

**Richard Parkin** was head of pensions policy at Fidelity International, one of Britain's biggest providers of private and workplace pensions. He spent 15 years at the company and remains a leading expert on pensions in Britain and other countries.

* * *

Annuities are still being bought, but in far smaller numbers and with much bigger pension pots. The average value of annuities purchased from company pension schemes has jumped from around £20,000 to around £50,000 since the pension freedoms were introduced.

It's interesting to note that annuities are generally bought by those who are at or even beyond their stated retirement age, whereas much of the other activity is happening a long time before retirement. Of those accessing their pension savings, nearly half had five years or more to go to their retirement date.

There's also another, less often mentioned change to the rules that came with the new freedoms, which was the taxation of pension savings when someone died. Now, pension pots left behind are almost invariably free of inheritance tax and may be free of tax altogether. This is leading people with other assets to use those first, so reducing the size of their estate.

In general, I expect people to start taking lump sums from their pensions in the run-up to retirement. They may continue to do this through retirement, perhaps to top up earned income or bridge the gap between retirement and when other pensions are paid. Finally, they may come back to annuities in later life if they need the income – but where they don't the pension pot will be passed on to the next generation.

But this all works because many of those accessing their pensions now have plenty of guaranteed income from final salary pension plans. Future retirees won't be so lucky.

## People will start buying annuities again

**Tom McPhail** is head of retirement policy for Hargreaves Lansdown, the stockbroker and investment platform, and is a leading pensions analyst and a contributor to government policy development on pensions.

\* \* \*

Pension freedoms have proved immensely popular and since they came into effect sales of annuities have dropped. This is not the same, though, as assuming that annuities don't have an essential role to play. Far from it: not only has annuity demand now stabilised, but I also expect it to increase again in the future.

Annuities perform a couple of essential jobs that very few other sources of income can deliver.

They provide a risk-free income, and they pay out for all of your life, however long that may be.

This means you don't have to worry about the economy slowing down, the stock market falling, dividends being cut or any other investment risk factor: whatever happens, you'll still get your income. It also means you have insurance against living too long.

Most of us go into retirement not knowing how long we need to make our savings last. This means we risk either running down our savings too fast, or not living well enough in retirement and then dying with unused savings in the bank. It is almost impossible to get this right on your own, but an annuity does exactly that for you automatically.

I would always recommend people to cover essential household expenditure needs with a secure income. For many this might be their state pension and perhaps some final salary income too. For anyone without enough guaranteed retirement income already, the logical choice is to use as much of their pension pot as necessary to buy that additional secure income through an annuity.

Once this secure income is in place, it becomes much easier and safer to keep the balance of your retirement savings invested for a mixture of growth and income, drawing variable income from the investments.

# Part Three

## Tax, Advice and Other Sources of Income

Like all our finances, pensions don't exist in isolation. The final part of this book covers the essentials that you'll need to know about tax and – if appropriate – using your home as a source of further income or capital. We also deal with advice: when you might need the help of a professional – and how much you should expect to pay for it.

# Chapter Seven
# What You Need to Know about Tax

**"How can I be sure I don't pay too much tax?"**

Previous chapters have aimed to help you control your pension pot and invest it appropriately. If you've got this far, congratulations.

Now you need a basic knowledge of the tax situation when you draw regular or one-off sums from your pension.

The bulk of this chapter looks at the tax treatment of withdrawals. It also looks at the tax risk that faces wealthy savers who might exceed the maximum amount you're allowed to build up within a pension during your lifetime.

We've written this chapter under a number of clear subject headings: if one or other does not apply to your circumstances, you can skip that section.

## The need to consider tax

In theory, the mechanics of taking money out of your pension pot as and when you need it should be simple.

The platform you have chosen will allow you to set up regular payments to transfer the dividends or other income earned from your pension account to your bank account.

Or, for one-off withdrawals, perhaps from the regular sale of holdings described in Chapter Five, you can simply transfer money manually from your pension to your current account on an occasional basis.

But before you make withdrawals you need to set up your pension in a way that takes account of – and makes the most of – the fact that you are entitled to take 25% of that pension pot tax-free. And that's where things get a little more complicated.

## Tax and pensions: the basic relationships

One of the biggest reasons to save into a pension in the first place is the fact that you receive income tax relief on your contributions. In other words, it's as if the money you pay in is not subject to income tax.

Someone who pays 20% basic-rate tax (who would take home £80 for every £100 earned after income tax) gets the following benefit when he or she saves into a pension: their £80 contribution is bumped up by 25% to become £100.

And someone who pays the 40% higher rate of tax (who would keep £60 for every £100 earned) gets the following benefit: their £60 contribution is bumped up by 67% to £100.

Wind the clock forward a few decades: you are now retired and you want to take money out of your pension.

In order to truly benefit from the pension system, you want to try to withdraw your pension at a lower rate of income tax than the rate of tax relief that you received when you contributed the money.

One winning scenario would be:

- You paid into your pension as a higher-rate taxpayer, collecting 40% tax relief.

- You take income out of the pension as a basic-rate taxpayer, paying only 20% tax.

Clearly, it is less satisfactory if you pay the same rate of tax on your pension income in retirement as you received in tax relief on your pension contributions while you were working. In that situation, the tax flows would cancel each other out. You have saved 20% tax when you contributed money to the pension while you were working, but you then pay 20% tax on your income from the pension when you have retired.

In this case, your only benefit would be the 25% lump sum: here you received full tax relief upfront but will pay no tax when you take the lump sum out. That's why the tax-free lump sum is so important. It needs to be cherished.

Once the tax-free lump sum has been taken, any withdrawals that you make from the remainder of your pension pot are subject to income tax just as if they were wages (although there is no National Insurance to pay on withdrawals from pensions).

Under current rules and allowances, everyone can receive £12,500 income per year and pay no tax on it at all. This is called the personal allowance. The next £37,500 attracts tax at 20%. Above that, income is taxed at 40%. There is a further *additional* rate of 45% on income over £150,000 in any one tax year. *Please note these allowances are subject to frequent change. Slightly different rates and bands apply in Scotland.*

The next few pages deal with this issue of the tax-free lump sum and the remaining, potentially taxable part of your pension pot. We explain:

1. The basics of your 25% tax-free entitlement.

2. How to take *all* the tax-free money at once, leaving the remaining 75% invested.

3. How to take *only part* of the tax-free money, leaving everything else invested.

4. How to take successive withdrawals where 25% is always tax-free and 75% always taxable.

5. What happens if you take money from your pension – but then want to put more in again at a later date.

6. How the tax is actually paid.

## 1. The basics of your 25% tax-free entitlement

Previous governments decided that when people retired they would need a lump sum of cash to set them off in this new stage of life, along with an income that would see them through the rest of their days. The two important principles here are:

1.  The lump sum would be free of tax.

2.  The income thereafter would be taxed, just as earned wages are taxed. Therefore, for income above the annual tax-free personal allowance, income tax is payable.

As we've covered in earlier chapters, the financial landscape facing retirees today is not quite as straightforward as for earlier generations.

But those basic principles remain. One quarter of your pension pot can be taken free of tax. And this is a very valuable perk for everyone.

How you maximise the value of your 25% tax-free portion very much depends on your circumstances. What you want to try to do, as much as possible, is spread your pension withdrawals so that you are not pushed into a higher tax bracket in any one year.

The following examples highlight various possibilities. All figures are for the 2019–20 tax year

### Scenario one: income needed now

**Q: I'm 56 and earn £17,000 a year in a part-time job. I plan to keep this job for the next two years, after which my mortgage will be cleared. I have a substantial pension pot of about £350,000. To help me through this period I want to take £15,000 a year from my pension pot, starting now. How much tax will I pay?**

Putting aside your entitlement to the 25% tax-free lump sum, you'll pay 20% income tax on all of your £15,000 pension income, , so you'll pay tax of £3,000. That's because your earned income of £17,000 already takes you above the £12,500 annual personal allowance.

### Scenario two: capital needed now

**Q: I'm 56 and earn £17,000 a year in a part-time job. I plan to keep this job for the next two years. I have a substantial pension pot of about £350,000. I want to take £80,000 out in a lump sum to help my son buy a house. How much tax will I pay?**

Putting aside your entitlement to the 25% tax-free lump sum, you'll pay 20% income tax on £33,000 of your pension withdrawal, and then 40% on £47,000.

Here's how it adds up: your £17,000 earned income uses up your full £12,500 personal allowance. You can take £33,000 of your £80,000 pension taxed at the basic rate of 20%, because you are allowed income of up to £50,000 while paying the 20% tax rate. Beyond that threshold, you pay the higher rate of tax, so the remaining £47,000 of your pension payment is taxed at the higher rate of 40%.

20% tax on £33,000 = £6,600

40% tax on £47,000 = £18,800

In total, you'll pay £25,400 tax on your £80,000 pension withdrawal.

*If the people in our scenarios made use of their 25% tax-free allowances, however, they could save a great deal of tax.*

In scenario one, the person could withdraw £30,000 from their pension tax-free, to get through the next two years. After that, he or she would no longer be working, but nor would there be a mortgage to pay. They could live on a smaller income where a higher proportion of their total income could then be set against their £12,500 personal allowance. They would still have some tax-free cash left to take as well.

In scenario two, the £80,000 should come from the tax-free lump sum. For all £80,000 to be tax-free, the pension pot would have to be £320,000 or more – but the aim would be to obtain as much of the £80,000 as possible from the tax-free portion, even if the pension pot were smaller. This would cut the £25,400 tax bill or even eliminate it.

While simplistic, these examples show that it is important to try to bear your pension in mind when it comes to major life events such as stopping paid work or making major one-off financial transactions.

*The tax-free lump sum plays a special part in this: it's your ticket to large one-off withdrawals from your pension pot.*

Married couples have further flexibility because they can each draw on their pension money at different times, with an eye to minimising their overall tax liability. The broad principle is that it is better for each of the couple to draw smaller sums from their pension in one year than for one person to draw one larger sum. This is especially the case where incomes are close to one of the tax thresholds.

For example, if a couple needs £24,000 to live on for a single year, it will be more efficient to try to arrange matters so that each withdraws £12,000 from their pension rather than one person withdrawing all £24,000.

Say Mrs Trellis takes the entire income of £24,000 from her pension. Beyond her £12,500 annual allowance, she will pay tax at 20%. So she pays 20% of £11,500, which is £2,300.

If Mr and Mrs Trellis can fix things so that each withdraws £12,000, they each pay no tax on just £150.

The arrangement would thus save them £2,300 in tax.

## 2. How to take all the tax-free money out at once, leaving the remaining 75% invested

Let's say your pension pot is worth £100,000. It's invested in one of the portfolios outlined in Chapter Four.

But now you want to access some of the money.

In the simplest scenario, you want just the £25,000 tax-free element encashed today, and to leave the rest invested.

This is a popular option. In many ways it follows the old pattern before the pension freedoms existed, when retirees would typically take the 25% lump sum and then spend the rest on an annuity, which would pay them an income for life. In this case, tax was payable only on the annuity income.

Now, though, we're more likely to be considering taking the 25% and then leaving the rest invested to provide a mix of income and growth for years to come.

This route is called *drawdown*. For once, here's a pension term that makes sense: most of your invested pension pot will be left untouched, from which future income and/or lump sums can be drawn down.

We outlined our tactics for working out how much you can safely draw down in Chapter Five.

## 3. How to take only part of the tax-free money and leave everything else invested – partial drawdown

There may be sound tax reasons not to take all of your 25% tax-free entitlement at once. This is particularly the case where savers have amassed larger pension pots.

Say your pension pot is worth £800,000. Let's recall the scenario above where the saver wanted to give their son £80,000 towards buying a house.

If you were in your late 50s and had a pension pot of £800,000, why encash all £200,000 (the maximum 25% tax-free lump sum) if the need was for only £80,000?

*Although there would be no income tax to pay on the £200,000 withdrawal, the money would then be outside the pension and lose the associated tax protection. Any future income or growth it generated would become liable to tax.*

To follow this scenario through, say you took £200,000 and, after giving your son £80,000, you had £120,000 remaining. As you have no immediate need for this money, you invest it alongside your pension money in exactly the same mix of funds. But the difference would be that the income and growth generated in future from this

£120,000 would have to be declared to the taxman, as it is no longer held in a tax-protected pension account.

Not only would you end up paying more tax, but you would have the considerable headache of having to calculate the tax liability.

The solution is to take *partial* or *phased* drawdown.

You start with £800,000 and, in this case, *you move £320,000 into drawdown*, which allows you to release £80,000 (the 25% tax-free lump sum from the £320,000) to give to your son. Your pension provider keeps a record of the fact that there is now £240,000 of your pension (£320,000 less £80,000) which no longer carries a tax-free cash entitlement. This money can remain invested, however, just as before.

The other, untouched element of your pension pot, of £480,000, still has the benefit of the 25% tax-free lump sum attached to it; this can be withdrawn in future.

## Those likely to benefit from partial drawdown

In theory you can enter into multiple, repeated processes like the one described above. The disadvantage is that it can create complexity in managing your overall pot of pension money.

Partial or phased drawdown is likely to be worth considering if you're younger, if you have a large pension pot and if you're still earning an income, or likely to earn again in future.

The latter point is important. As you will see below, there are specific rules that apply to how much you can pay into a pension once you have taken some money out of it. Broadly speaking, if all you have taken out is your tax-free lump sum, you can continue to pay into your pension under the normal rules.

But if you have drawn income from the main, taxed portion of your pension, your ability to contribute in future is much reduced. If you are still earning and able to put some money into your pension, you need to be careful not to limit that ability by any actions you take early on in the years beyond age 55.

The rules relating to contributions in these circumstances are explained more fully in point 5 on page 118.

## 4. How to take successive withdrawals where 25% is always tax-free

What if you wish to make successive withdrawals where 25% is always tax-free and 75% is taxed?

This process is known as UFPLS – see the jargon buster below – and has as its main benefit an element of simplicity.

Here, every time you make a withdrawal from your pension pot, 25% of that withdrawal is tax-free and 75% is taxed.

But, as you will have gathered from reading the above points, this is not necessarily very helpful, because it does not allow for much planning. Think back to our case study who wanted to take £80,000 tax-free out of their pension pot to help a child buy a home.

In some cases, UFPLS may suit those with smaller pension pots who wish to encash the entire pot all at once. Such a scenario isn't likely to arise among readers of this book, who are expecting to continue investing most or all of their pension for some years into the future.

The major downside is that as 75% of every withdrawal is potentially taxable, you are limiting yourself to smaller withdrawals only – or exposing yourself to the risk of paying unnecessary tax.

The second disadvantage – see below – is that it much reduces your ability to contribute further into a pension in future.

## Jargon buster: What on earth does UFPLS mean?

While drawdown is a logical term that describes what's happening to your pension money, the horrible term UFPLS is meaningless. It stands for *uncrystallised funds pension lump sum*. It describes a process where every slice of pension withdrawn is treated as a mini-pension, with 25% of the withdrawal being tax-free and 75% liable to tax.

**The three different ways of taking cash from your pension**

**1.**
Take the whole 25% tax-free sum at once, leaving the other 75% invested: drawdown.

**2.**
Take just part of your 25% tax-free sum, leaving everything else invested: partial drawdown.

**3.**
Take successive withdrawals, where each time 25% is tax-free: UFPLS.

## 5. What happens if you take money from your pension – but then want to put more in again at a later date:

While technically we can all now get hold of our pension savings from age 55, many of us won't want to stop working at such an early age – and many won't be able to afford to. What's likely to happen in most people's lives is that their pension, earnings and other savings all play a combined part for some years in meeting a range of financial objectives.

Tax is a major consideration here.

After your home, your pension is likely to be your biggest asset. So it is natural that you might wish to turn to it to provide a lump sum while you remain in your 50s or 60s.

Earlier in this chapter we raised the scenario of a well-off pension saver wishing to access their pension pot to give a child £80,000 towards buying a house. But you might want to use money inside a pension to pay for a child's university education. Or to clear your own mortgage.

Having used the pension to provide this lump sum, you may still fully intend to continue working for a decade or more, during which time you will want to replenish the pension pot and take advantage of the generous tax relief available in doing so. The rules around this are changing.

Once you have accessed pension money (over and above the 25% tax-free element), you are restricted to contributing a total of £4,000 into a pension each tax year.

By contrast, if all you have done is take tax-free money under your 25% lump sum entitlement, you are able to contribute up to the usual allowance, which for almost everyone is £40,000 per year, including your company's contributions.

If you are taking cash from your pension while still planning to continue working and contributing further to your pension in the years ahead, you should consider using drawdown and withdrawing only your tax-free entitlement.

*Let's look at an example to illustrate this.*

Gary is 62 and has previously used partial drawdown to encash £30,000 of his £300,000 pension pot. Last year, he took 25% of the £30,000 (£7,500) as a tax-free lump sum to pay for refurbishments to his kitchen, and left the remainder (£22,500) in his pension. He then decided to go back to work as a business consultant for two years when aged 63, and earns £100,000 a year. Out of that money, he is able to continue to make contributions to his pension, up to a maximum of £40,000 per year, because he has not yet taken any of the taxable portion of his pension.

Conversely, if Gary had followed the UFPLS process, and withdrawn the full £30,000, paying no tax on 25% of it and subjecting 75% of it to tax, he would have started taking taxable benefits from his pension pot and he would now be limited to paying a maximum of £4,000 a year of new money into his pension.

---

## Jargon buster: What on earth is the MPAA?

MPAA stands for *money purchase annual allowance*, another tongue-twisting, brain-curdling invention of the pensions world. This describes the reduced annual contribution limit to pensions that applies once someone has dipped into the taxable part of their pension.

---

## 6. When I take money from my pension, how is the tax actually paid?

Very often you arrive at an understanding of how tax works in theory. Then, in practice, when the deductions are being made or HMRC is asking for certain pieces of information, it all becomes incomprehensible again.

It's worth knowing what to expect when you make withdrawals.

Firstly, if all you're taking is tax-free money, you'll pay nothing in tax. That part is rather obvious!

When you start to make withdrawals outside your 25% tax-free entitlement, however, you will be subject to tax as if the money was earned income. In this case, your pension provider will perform similar functions to an employer under the pay-as-you-earn (PAYE) system. It will obtain a tax code from HMRC, and it will apply this to the money you withdraw.

The first time this happens your provider might need to apply an emergency tax code, which may mean too little or too much tax is deducted. You will need to look carefully at your statement and check with HMRC where you suspect errors.

If your first taxable withdrawal is made shortly after you leave employment, or while you're still working, send your pension provider details of your tax code from your P45 or P60.

You can check how much tax you're paying using the 'Check your income tax for the current year' service available on www.gov.uk. You'll need to be registered with the Government Gateway, the official portal for various purposes, which involves strict identity verification, to do this.

Once a pension payment has been made to you, your provider should be sent an updated code by HMRC. Payments thereafter should be taxed more accurately.

Because the pension freedoms are relatively new, it is not yet clear how well HMRC – already battling to apply a highly complex tax regime – is succeeding in accurately taxing withdrawals.

Those who make regular withdrawals from their pension pots are less likely to suffer errors – or, at least, they should be easier to correct once spotted.

If you're making ad hoc withdrawals, however, it is a good idea to keep a close eye on how much tax you are paying, on those withdrawals individually and for that year in total.

## The lifetime allowance

This section is for people with large or multiple pensions. If your pension pot is approaching £1m, or likely to reach that value in future, you should read this. You should also read it if you have a generous final salary pension income from one or more jobs. Otherwise you can skip this section.

*What is the lifetime allowance?*

The lifetime allowance is a fixed sum above which the value of all your pension savings is not allowed to rise during the course of your life. First set at £1.8m, it has fallen steadily. In April 2014 it fell to £1.25m and in April 2016 it was cut again to £1m. It then rose slightly, in line with inflation, to £1.055m for the tax year 2019–20.

*How do I work out if my pensions are at risk of exceeding the lifetime limit?*

It's not that easy, in practice. If you have gone through the processes outlined in previous chapters you should have a good idea of the value of your total pension pot. If it is with one provider, it equates to your total balance.

But many people for whom the lifetime allowance is a risk will also have other final-salary type pensions, whose value (for the purpose of the lifetime allowance) is calculated in a different way.

Broadly speaking, you multiply the initial annual income to which you are entitled under such schemes by 20 in order to obtain a value of the pension for the purposes of the lifetime allowance.

*Here's a simple example.*

You have a pension pot, from which you have yet to take any benefits, worth £620,000. You also have an entitlement to two different final salary pensions, which will pay you a starting pension of £7,000 and £3,200 per year respectively.

You add £620,000 to £140,000 (20 x £7,000) and £64,000 (20 x £3,200). Any additional tax-free lump sums to which you are entitled from your final salary pensions must be added on top. We will assume none applies here. Your state pension entitlement isn't included. That makes a total of £824,000.

In this case, depending on your age and other circumstances, you may have some cause to worry that in due course your savings will break through the limit – even if you do not contribute further money to your pension. Strong investment growth on its own could push you above the allowance. You may need to take action.

*How does the taxman check whether I've exceeded the limit?*

There are several key triggers when your pension provider will apply a lifetime allowance check. The main ones are:

- If you use some or all of your pension money to buy an annuity before age 75.

- If you move your pension pot into a drawdown arrangement before age 75.

- If you take a lump sum out of your pension pot without being in a drawdown arrangement, while under age 75.

- If you die before age 75 and your spouse or other beneficiary does any of the above.

- When you reach the age of 75.

*What penalties apply if I exceed the allowance?*

Higher rates of tax apply. Your provider will apply a high 55% rate of tax to the excess when it is drawn from the pension as a one-off sum, or 25% tax if you take it as income.

In an ideal world, a pension saver would detect the risk and avoid exceeding the allowance. The worst-case scenario is where more contributions are being made to a large pension and these contributions are themselves responsible for pushing it above the threshold.

Less disastrous is the scenario in which successful investment returns drive the value of the pot above the limit: in this case you are not losing money, you are simply keeping less of the gain made on it.

In any case, you may be able to successfully avoid the tax penalties by applying for 'protection' allowed for in the law – see below.

*What action can I take?*

The most obvious action to avoid exceeding the allowance is to stop contributing to your pension when the risk emerges. If that's not enough, you could also withdraw money to ensure you remain below the limit. You may pay tax when you do this, but not as much as you would if you allowed the pot to breach the lifetime allowance.

For those in final salary pension arrangements where benefits are still being accrued, you could consider retiring early (this is typically likely to apply only to senior civil servants, NHS employees and a handful of other groups).

You can also boost your lifetime allowance by taking out 'protection'. There are several types, but these are the two you're most likely to use:

### 1. Fixed protection 2016

This locks your lifetime allowance at £1.25m (its level before April 2016). But if you obtain this protection you can no longer put any money into any pension arrangement. Nor can your employer. Your invested pensions can however continue to grow up to that higher limit.

### 2. Individual protection 2016

This locks your lifetime allowance to the lower of the two following figures: the total value of your pension(s) at 5 April 2016 or £1.25m.

In other words, this works only for those whose pensions were above the £1.25m limit in April 2016. You are technically permitted to continue contributing to your pension, but in practice your opportunities to do so will be very limited.

Both of the above get-outs are useful for well-off savers, and mean that in many cases tax penalties can be avoided. There is no set deadline by when these protections need to be applied for. But the more time that passes, the less useful they become.

If you discover that you have exceeded the limit already and have been making further contributions since April 2016, you are likely to need professional help. See Chapter Eleven for more on where to find such help and how much it might cost.

## Finally, a note on buy-to-let

An estimated two million people own properties in addition to their home, which they let out. Many are doubtless counting on the rental income to help them through retirement. Some will have built portfolios of buy-to-let properties specifically to generate retirement income.

The scope of this book doesn't stretch to the pros and cons of buy-to-let. While certain types of pension allow investors to hold commercial property, residential property is not allowed inside a pension. Buy-to-let is not therefore core to the subject of how to manage and invest your pension assets.

But in relation to tax, there are a number of points to consider when looking at the issue of whether money saved up inside a pension should be taken out and used in other investments, notably buy-to-let.

Here is a question *Telegraph* readers often ask:

Q: "Wouldn't it be a good idea to take money out of my pension and invest it in a buy-to-let property?"

The answer, broadly speaking, is no. Putting aside the risks, costs and practical difficulties inherent in managing a property, and putting aside the comparatively low yields now offered by residential property in many regions, there are some serious tax disadvantages in undertaking this course of action.

With a pension:

- Income generated by the investments inside the pension is tax-free.

- Capital growth of the investments inside the pension is tax-free.

- The pension assets can be passed on at death free of inheritance tax.

With a buy-to-let:

- Rental income is subject to tax along with all your other income.

- Capital gains on the property are taxed at the highest rates of capital gains tax.

- The buy-to-let properties will form part of your estate and so be liable to inheritance tax.

Earlier parts of this chapter have raised the question of what you would do with money removed from inside a pension if you did not have an immediate need to spend it or give it away.

The problem is that the pension offers good protection from tax while assets remain within it. Once outside, any returns and growth generated by the money are likely to be taxable. With buy-to-let, which is taxed differently from other investments, this is especially the case.

If you have enough money in your pension pot to be able to withdraw a sum sufficient to buy a property, you are likely to need to think about inheritance tax. Buy-to-let is particularly inefficient from this point of view.

Inheritance tax – and the value of your pension as a way to limit it – is the subject of the next chapter.

---

## HMRC can take huge amounts of tax from pension withdrawals

**Steve Webb**, former pensions minister and director of policy at Royal London, the insurer.

\* \* \*

One of the unexpected (and rather unwelcome) features of the new pension freedoms has been the way HMRC has chosen to administer the deduction of tax from initial pension withdrawals.

Beyond any tax-free lump sum, pension withdrawals are taxed as income in the year in which they are taken. A large withdrawal in one go can see someone drawn into the 40% or 45% tax bracket. This is one of a number of reasons why spreading withdrawals over several years rather than taking them in a lump sum can be a good idea.

For regular taxable income such as wages or regular pension payments, HMRC operates a pay-as-you-earn (PAYE) system which tries to smooth your tax bill over the course of the year. Each month, HMRC looks at how much taxable income you have received so far that year and looks at how much tax-free allowance you are entitled to in that year, and works out your tax bill accordingly.

This is known as a cumulative tax assessment. For most people, it results in paying the correct amount of tax with no end-year adjustment.

But for many people who take taxable cash under the pension freedoms, this is not how the system works. Unless your pension provider already has a PAYE tax code for you, it will deduct tax using an emergency tax code for all but the smallest withdrawals.

Under this emergency or non-cumulative system, you are treated as if you were going to make a similar withdrawal every month of the year. Not surprisingly, this assumption would take most people well into the higher tax brackets, and a big tax bill is the result.

In the long run, this problem should be sorted out. You can apply at once to claim back any overpaid tax and if you do not do this HMRC maintains that it will all be sorted out by a reconciliation process at the end of the year. But if you want the full value of your pension withdrawal now, you are unlikely to be very happy to see a large tax deduction that you then have to claim back.

One possible way round this problem is to make a nominal withdrawal – for example, just £1 – before the one you actually want to make. This process is likely to trigger HMRC to issue a regular tax code to your pension provider and subsequent withdrawals can then be made on the more normal (cumulative) basis.

In my view it is an absurdity knowingly to overtax savers and leave it to them to claim back their overpaid tax. If emergency tax codes are needed, the right thing to do would surely be for HMRC to deduct basic-rate tax at source in all cases. This would get the tax bill right for most people. For high earners any taxable withdrawals could be declared on their tax return and any additional tax due could then be collected.

HMRC should not be allowed to get away with overtaxing people simply because it is more convenient for the taxman.

# Chapter Eight
# What Happens to Your Pensions When You Die

**"How can I be sure my family benefits as much as possible when I die?"**

In Chapter Seven we covered the must-know basics about how much tax you are likely to pay when you draw money from your pension.

In this chapter we look at what happens to leftover pension money when you die. This is important because an understanding of this issue could mean you change the way you use your different pots of savings during retirement in order to deliver better tax outcomes for your family or other heirs.

## The difference between your pension pot and a pension income

First, let's have a quick reminder of a distinction we made in Chapter One. When people talk about a pension, they are often referring to a regular retirement income, such as is paid by an annuity or the state pension. A quite different concept is your pension pot: money stored in a pension account in the form of cash, shares or other investments.

*When you die these different forms of pension work very differently.*

Regular income from an annuity or final salary pension might continue to be paid to your spouse or partner after your death. They might receive all the income or (much more commonly) they might receive half or two-thirds of the former monthly sum.

This depends entirely on the type of annuity you entered into or the terms stipulated in your final salary pension. If and when you plan ahead for the eventuality of your death, you need to note what your surviving spouse can expect to receive from these arrangements. This has always been the case.

By contrast, the issue of bequeathing a pension pot is somewhat new. It is also likely to become far more common as more people choose to manage their pension cash into retirement along the lines laid out in this book.

## Inheritance tax and your pension pot

One of the most significant elements of George Osborne's changes to the pension regime was to scrap the death tax that applied to pension assets. There was never inheritance tax to pay for those inheriting a pension pot, but Osborne's reforms saw the end of a separate tax on pensions that had the same effect.

This provides a huge benefit to the better-off. It's also a great incentive to leave pension assets intact within the pension pot – rather than turn them into an income by, for instance, purchasing an annuity.

Inheritance tax is relatively simple. Each person has an *exemption*, or *nil-rate band*, of £325,000, which they can leave to their beneficiaries free of tax. Married couples and civil partners can add their exemptions together and leave a combined £650,000 tax-free. (There is also a further allowance that applies to the family home which is currently being phased in by the government.)

Above those thresholds, an estate is taxed at 40%.

Pension pots enjoy unique tax treatment, different from a family home or your other savings and investments. Because of this, there are tax implications relating to the order in which you spend or give away your various assets.

Take the scenario outlined by this fortunate *Telegraph* reader, who wrote in for advice:

> Q: I am a widow managing to get by on my state pension and a small company pension paid to me following my husband's death. My husband also left £330,000 in a pension account managed by his stockbroker. I have £200,000 in ISAs. I am not sure what to do with these. I live in an expensive part of Surrey and estimate my house to be worth at least £1m, so I am worried about inheritance tax and want to leave as much as possible to my two daughters. I am 82.

The value of her property means this woman's estate is going to be liable to some inheritance tax whatever she does. But she could certainly take steps to limit the potential tax due on the other assets, thanks to the pension pot being free of any inheritance tax liability.

Because she can bequeath the full £330,000 pension pot to her children free of inheritance tax at her death, she should keep that money intact. It can remain invested relatively "aggressively" – largely in shares, for example, as opposed to cash – depending on the age of her daughters and their own needs for the money.

Let's assume she's taken on her husband's £325,000 nil-rate band allowance, which in addition to her own gives £650,000. There may also, depending on the year of her death, be a further exemption applying to her home. But for now let's assume that of her total £1.2m non-pension assets (house at £1m and £200,000 in ISAs), the value above the combined nil-rate bands of £650,000 will be taxed at 40%.

The £200,000 ISA savings will thus be liable to a 40% tax charge. If she needs to spend money on herself, supplementing her income or paying for care, for instance, she should use this ISA cash before touching the pension.

Alternatively, if she has no need for the £200,000 ISA money, she could immediately give it to her two daughters, taking advantage of what is known as the seven-year rule. This rule allows assets to fall outside the estate for inheritance tax purposes provided that the giver (or what the taxman calls the donor) survives for seven years after making the gift. If she used the money in her pension instead she would forfeit the ability to leave it to her children free of inheritance tax after her death. She would also have to withdraw the money from the pension before she gave it to her daughters, and this would incur a tax charge.

As you can see, there is an incentive for those people whose overall assets exceed the nil-rate band to use their pension savings as a last resort, and to spend other savings first, in order to leave more tax-free inheritance for their heirs.

Taking this argument to its extreme, some financial planners might even suggest that the woman above – or others in similar situations – consider borrowing money against their home. Doing so reduces the value of the property for inheritance tax purposes and frees up cash which could be given to beneficiaries right away or spent, for instance, on the woman's care in later life. The pension then becomes the biggest single asset, which is able to be passed on free of tax.

There are a number of risks to borrowing later in life, however, and you should always seek professional advice before undertaking such a strategy. These risks are looked at in more detail in Chapter Ten.

## Thinking ahead about what will happen to your pension after your death

As a starting point, nominate who you wish to inherit your pension, by formally lodging that information with your pension provider.

Just because your pension pot isn't taxed in the same way as the rest of your estate, it doesn't follow that your heirs can get their hands on it entirely tax-free.

In general, this is how the recipients of your pension pot will be taxed:

• If you die *before* age 75 and leave a pension pot, the recipients of your pension pot will be able to take the money tax-free.

- If you die at *age 75 or over* and leave a pension pot, the recipients will be taxed on withdrawals from that pension at their own rate of income tax. They do not have to be over age 55 to make withdrawals.

Just as you would want to manage your pension withdrawals to minimise income tax (see Chapter Six), so your spouse, children or other beneficiaries might need to do the same when it comes to accessing the pension pot you leave them.

The rules also allow pots to be passed on more than once. Say you die, and your wife or husband takes ownership of your pot. Any of the money that is unspent in the remainder of their life can remain within the pension and can pass on again to your children or other beneficiaries.

## Cashing in your final salary pension benefits in order to bequeath them

In Chapters One and Two we described in some detail how final salary pensions work and why they are so valuable. In most cases you would not want to encash these entitlements.

If you have reached retirement age and started to take the final salary pension income you are not likely to have any choice in the matter in any case. But if you have yet to start taking income from a final salary scheme you may be able to take cash instead. The amount you would get is called the *transfer value*.

The final salary pension administrator will undertake a calculation to place a lump sum value on the lifetime income you would receive if you were to draw your final salary pension as an income in the normal way. It will then produce the transfer value figure, which is the cash payment the administrator will offer you to leave the scheme and give up the promised pension income. This is a complex process.

When the transfer value is presented to you, if it is £30,000 or more then you are required to take financial advice by law. This is because the authorities want to ensure that anyone who takes this irreversible step is fully aware of the risks.

But there may be circumstances in which the lump sum is far more valuable.

Here is a real-life scenario based on the case of a *Telegraph* reader:

> Jonathan, in his early fifties, was in generally poor health and not working. He would have to wait until his pension scheme retirement age of 62 before he could take a final salary pension built up in his former employment. This would pay an income of around £12,000 a year, linked to inflation. Or he could take a cash transfer of £326,000 now.
>
> His poor health was part of the reason to opt for the cash, as reduced life expectancy reduces the value of an income that lasts as long as you live. But he also had other investments producing an income in the form of two properties. His younger partner, to whom he was not married, was also able to support him financially. This meant his need for future income from this pension was relatively low.
>
> The value of the cash lump sum, however, especially as it could be bequeathed to his partner without inheritance tax, was more significant.
>
> In this case he chose to go ahead with the transfer. The money went into a pension pot where it was invested in a range of funds. If he needs to, Jonathan can access this money once he is 55. Otherwise it can remain invested.

# Chapter Nine
# Your State Pension

**"How do I make my state pension go further?"**

If you have managed to save a decent amount for retirement, you may think that the state pension is almost an irrelevance. But if you look at the size of the lump sum you'd need to replace it, you'll see that it's a very significant amount.

The state pension may also be your only source of guaranteed, index-linked income for life. It's therefore important to check that you are in line to receive the full payment – and to be prepared to take action if not.

## Check your state pension entitlement

So far our aim has been to help you to get the most out of your own retirement savings. But it's important not to forget the other significant source of income in later life: the state pension.

The state pension can get a bad press; it is often criticised as inadequate. But some of this criticism misses the point. Yes, on its own the state pension is not enough for most people. However, it can still make a huge contribution to your total income. Better still, it is guaranteed, involves no risk (you are not investing the money yourself) and it rises in line with inflation every year.

We think it's best to view the state pension as a vital pillar of your retirement income. As such, it's worth putting considerable effort into ensuring that you will receive the maximum amount possible, because the rules are complex and even small mistakes could result in a significant reduction in what you get.

Crucially, you should check as early as possible that you are on track to receive the maximum entitlement – don't leave it until you are on the point of retirement.

*In fact, check right now.*

Here, in seven questions and answers, we explain how to do this and cover all the key angles of the state pension and the part it plays in your retirement income plans.

## 1. How valuable is the state pension?

Under a new system that took effect in April 2015, anyone who retires after that date receives a *flat-rate* state pension – £168.60 for the 2019–20 tax year – if they have made enough National Insurance contributions. The system is called flat-rate because previously the state pension consisted of two parts: a basic pension and various top-ups, which included the State Earnings Related Pension Scheme (SERPS).

However, the flat-rate description can be misleading because it implies that everyone gets the same. In fact, not everyone will get the same because of complications designed to ensure that people who would have received more under the old system do not lose out – and that people who did not make full National Insurance contributions do not unfairly benefit.

However, if you are entitled to the full weekly amount, you will get an annual income from the state of £8,790 (in 2019–20) – which, don't forget, will rise every year in line with inflation. To get a sense of how valuable this secure, rising income is, we can look at how much it would cost to buy that same income on the annuity market.

At the time of writing, you would need to hand a lump sum of £273,000 to an annuity company in return for an inflation-linked equivalent income for life from age 65.

In other words, the value of the state pension when converted to a single sum is almost certainly significant in relation to your own overall pot.

It's important to remember that the state pension is taxable, in that it forms part of your taxable income. However, confusion often arises because the government normally pays it without deduction of tax. This is because the annual state pension is normally less than the tax-free annual allowance (£12,500 in the 2019–20 tax year). As a result, anyone whose only income is the state pension does indeed have no tax to pay.

However, it often doesn't take much income on top of the state pension to push people into the basic-rate tax bracket. Tax codes for pensioners are normally adjusted to take account of the taxable status of the state pension, but it's important to check that your tax code is right. There is advice on how to do this on the website of the Low Incomes Tax Reform Group: www.litrg.org.uk/tax-guides/pensioners.

## 2. How can I find out about my own entitlement?

The government can tell you how much you are on track to receive in state pension. There are several ways to get a forecast:

- Online at: www.gov.uk/check-state-pension

- By phone on: 0800 731 0175 or 0191 218 3600

- By post to: The Pension Service 9, Mail Handling Site A, Wolverhampton WV98 1LU

We have tried the online service and received our forecasts within minutes, with no fuss. There is also a complete breakdown of your National Insurance (NI) record to date, showing any years in which your contributions were incomplete and indicating where you may still be able to make them up now.

The forecast will state that it is based on the assumption that you will continue to work until your state pension age, although no one accrues more state pension entitlement after they have 35 years of full NI contributions (based on the law as it stands).

If you spot anything that doesn't look right in your NI record, it's best to call the service to double check that you really are entitled to the full amount, or whether there is any scope for filling the gaps in your record.

## 3. When will I receive the state pension?

For years the answer to this question was simple: 65 for men, 60 for women. Now things are changing.

Men and women already receive the state pension at the same age and the state pension age is now rising for both sexes. The process is gradual, so many people will find themselves retiring at the age of, say, 65 and six months.

In summary, the state pension age for men and women will increase to 67 between 2026 and 2028. There is a detailed table, which will show the retirement date for your own birthday, at www.tinyurl.com/newdkd6.

## 4. Is there any way to get more state pension?

There are two ways in which you may be able to increase what you get. The first, as we mentioned, is to make additional National Insurance contributions if your record is not complete.

But don't assume that you should automatically do this if you have some incomplete or missing years – the only thing that matters is having 35 full years of NI contributions by the time you are eligible to claim the state pension. If you are on course to do this, it would be a waste of money to buy the missing years.

If you do need to make up some missing years, you can make additional voluntary National Insurance contributions. HMRC has extended the usual deadlines for making these voluntary contributions for the tax years from 2006–7 to 2015–16 – you will have until 5 April 2023 to make the contributions, so you don't need to decide now. You should contact HMRC to make the payments.

The other way to increase your annual state pension is to put off claiming it. For each year you delay, the pension rises by just under 5.8%.

This may sound like a good idea, but it does mean that you will, in the end, receive the pension for one year fewer than otherwise. This has to be balanced against the fact that the annual pension will be higher for your entire retirement.

Broadly speaking, the longer you live, the greater the benefit of deferring.

After all, if you were unlucky enough to die one year after taking the state pension, and had delayed by a year, you would have received one year's pension instead of two in total, in exchange for 5.8% more in the one year – clearly a terrible deal.

At the other end of the scale, imagine that you live long enough to claim your state pension for 35 years. If you don't defer, the total amount you receive over the course of your retirement is £291,200 (disregarding inflation for simplicity's sake). If you defer for one year and claim the pension for 34 years instead, you'll get just under £300,000 in total – about £8,800 more.

If you don't want to take what amounts to a bet on your longevity, there is another option for those who could afford to defer: you simply claim the pension as soon as you are eligible and add it to your own pension pot instead of spending it. This gives you a good outcome either way: if you live for a long time and your pension investments perform well you will get as much in total as you would by deferring (or possibly more), thanks to investment growth on the first year's state pension income. But if you die early, you don't lose that first year's income.

## 5. I plan to retire at 60, several years before I receive the state pension. How do I bridge the gap?

As we have explained, the guaranteed, index-linked state pension is a benefit of great significance for all but the richest savers. But this very fact can complicate matters for some people, especially those who retire before or after the state pension date.

Let's imagine that you have accumulated a decent pot of pension savings by the age of 60 and decide to retire then. You will need that pension pot to produce all your income for the next five, six or seven years (the exact period will depend on your age, thanks to the increases in the state pension age), and then a reduced income once you start to receive the state pension.

How can you ensure that the pot produces the income you need for those first few years while at the same time ensuring that there is the right amount left when the second period begins? When, in other words, the role of your personal savings pot changes from providing all your income to augmenting what you receive from the state pension?

There are various ways to answer this question, but we believe the simplest is to establish the sum that needs to remain in your pension pot at the point that you start to receive your state pension and then tailor your withdrawals in the years before that point to achieve that sum. (If this tailoring results in the income being less than you need, the sums are telling you that you can't really afford to retire so early after all!)

## How do you establish this figure?

First, establish how much income you'll need in retirement, using the steps outlined on page 73 in Chapter Four. Subtract from that figure the income you will get from the state pension to arrive at the amount that needs to be generated by your pension pot. Decide which of our three portfolios suits you best in terms of the balance between income for you during your lifetime and your wish to leave money to others when you die, then use the percentage income from that portfolio to arrive at the capital sum needed.

For the 5% portfolio, multiply the annual income you need by 20. For the 4% portfolio multiply by 25 and for the 3% portfolio multiply by 33.

For example, let's assume that your budgeting exercise shows that you will need £25,000 a year. Deduct the state pension, roughly £8,700 (but use your own figure if your state pension forecast gave a different one), to arrive at £16,300 as the sum that needs to be generated by your investments.

To generate this annual income will require a pension pot of £326,000 if you use the high-income (5%) portfolio, £407,000 with the compromise (4%) portfolio and £538,000 from the inheritance (3%) portfolio.

But you should also increase these figures to account for inflation. If you will receive the state pension in five years' time, for example, assume an inflation rate of 2.5% and use an online calculator (there is one at www.calculator.net/inflation-calculator.html) to discover the inflation-adjusted figure. For example, £326,000 today is equivalent to £370,000 in five years' time – so this last figure would be the one to aim for.

The last step is to watch your rate of spending during those years between retirement and receiving the state pension to ensure that the value of your pension pot declines roughly at the rate required to meet the target value at the latter point.

## 6. I want to carry on working after the state pension age. How does this affect my pension planning?

If you are thinking of carrying on in work after the state pension age, you may wonder how this affects your state pension planning.

This depends to some extent on why you want to carry on working. If you are doing so because you think you can't afford to retire, eligibility to receive the state pension is likely to make a big difference.

As we discussed above, you have the choice of claiming your state pension straightaway or deferring it in exchange for an increase of about 5.8% a year.

Assuming that your financial situation is not causing you current difficulty as long as you carry on working, in other words that you don't need the state pension income to support your living expenses now, you could choose to defer, perhaps for several years.

This would give you a bigger state pension when you do eventually retire. However, as mentioned above, the other way is to claim the pension anyway and simply add it to your existing savings. This deals with the danger of dying early and receiving less, or nothing, of the state pension you are entitled to.

If you consider the effect of this on the amount you are saving and then take into account the fact that each year of extended working life reduces the size of the pension pot you will need for your shortened retirement – and the fact that once you reach state pension age you don't pay National Insurance contributions, even if you continue to work – you can see that prolonging your career changes significantly the balance between what you need and what you have, so with luck your retirement will not be long delayed.

A third possibility is taking the state pension and using the additional income to cut the number of hours you work, while you continue to save for the time when you can retire fully.

If, on the other hand, continuing to work is a choice rather than a necessity, you still have the options of deferring or claiming. Again, to avoid the danger of getting a poor return from your state pension should you die relatively early, you might consider claiming the pension anyway and adding the money to your pension pot. But do consider the tax implications of boosting your income in this way.

## 7. What about the threat to the state pension triple lock?

The *triple lock* is a commitment made by the government in 2010 to increase the state pension every year in line with the higher of price inflation or wage inflation, subject to a minimum in any event of 2.5%.

This is seen as a very valuable guarantee for pensioners. The other side of the coin is that the promise is expensive for the government. As a result there have been persistent fears that the triple lock will be scrapped or watered down.

If this were to happen, it would make the state pension less valuable over the course of a retirement, which implies that savers should accumulate a bigger pot of their own pension money to compensate.

However, politicians will tread warily: upsetting pensioners can cost a lot of votes. We think the most likely outcome is that the triple lock will be weakened slightly by removing the 2.5% floor to increases. In recent years, when inflation has been low, this element of the guarantee has been called into play, but there are likely to be many occasions when price or wage rises are higher. Scrapping the 2.5% floor is therefore unlikely to make too much difference to your eventual income.

## The state pension is vital – so check your entitlement regularly

**Ros Altmann** is an economist, long-standing pensions campaigner and former pensions minister.

\* \* \*

The word pension covers two separate concepts. Firstly, state pensions provide income that ensures citizens are not abandoned into poverty in retirement.

Secondly, private pensions are long-term investments that can provide extra money for spending in later life. The amount you receive depends on how much is paid in, interest rates and investment returns, so higher earners tend to have more.

Britain's state pension is a crucial part of most people's retirement income. A full state pension under the new single-tier system promises around £24 a day from pension age – just enough to avoid poverty. If you want more than this you need private pensions or other assets. Regardless of previous earnings, a bedrock of guaranteed, taxpayer-funded lifelong income can be an important base on to which people can build extra private income.

The new state pension has no earnings-related payments; the amount paid depends on the number of years of NI contributions. Of course, as working life and life expectancy change, NI rules covering elements such as state pension starting age, number of years of contributions needed for a full pension, or the amount or structure of the state pension itself, will change over time.

It is therefore vital to ensure that people know how the state pension works. Unfortunately, governments have not always properly informed people about rule changes.

For example, a few years ago, before I became pensions minister, I received a letter from the Department for Work & Pensions informing me that I had achieved the 30 years' NI contributions required for a full state pension. But at that very time legislation was going through Parliament to increase the required number of years to 35. Of course, I knew this because I was involved in pensions, but most people would have had no idea and would find out only years later that their NI record was incomplete.

Far worse than this, after changing the law in 1995 to significantly increase future state pension ages of women then in their 40s, governments failed to ensure that those women all knew that they would have to wait longer for their state pension. Many are now facing real hardship because they are not receiving their state pension when they expected to.

You should check your expected state pension entitlement and NI record regularly – every couple of years perhaps – to help you plan your future retirement income.

Some say the state pension in its current form will not be around for future generations, but I disagree. Means-testing state pensions undermines incentives to save, thus reducing future private provision. Having a base of income from the state above means-tested poverty levels ensures that people have clear incentives to save for their own retirement to supplement the state pension.

There is, however, one glaring omission from 21st century retirement social welfare: NI does not cover social care costs. One in four elderly people will need paid-for care, so national pooling of risk makes sense. But successive governments have ducked this difficult decision and failed to set aside money for care funding. Billions of pounds are earmarked for pensions, but nothing for later-life care. This crisis is worsening and needs urgent solutions to ensure dignity for millions of vulnerable elderly people in future.

# Chapter Ten
# Your Home as a Source of Cash

**"My home is my biggest asset: should I be using it somehow to fund my retirement?"**

Previous chapters have looked at your pension wealth, whether it's in the form of your investments, or an income from an annuity or your state pension.

But what if that's not enough? In that case, another obvious asset to tap is your home.

## Equity release

The process of taking money out of your home in later life is broadly described by the catch-all term *equity release*. The majority of equity release mortgages are available to borrowers aged over 55 or 60. Qualifying homeowners already supplement their retirement income by drawing equity from their properties in this way to the tune of several billion pounds per year. This is a trend that's expected to grow fast.

But borrowing in later life is a big decision. You are draining value from an asset which you have spent a large part of your working life paying for. There are implications not only for your own future, but also for your children or other heirs. There are tax considerations, too, and most importantly, there is the cost of the debt to take into account. Despite the sharp fall in interest rates, this type of borrowing is still expensive.

*Where possible, borrowing against your home in retirement as a means of topping up income is generally best avoided.*

If it is still something you are determined to consider, there are several types of mortgage that will help you to do this. These different types of mortgage arrangement are covered below in answering the following commonly asked questions about equity release.

- I'm in my 60s – how much can I borrow?

- How much will this borrowing cost me, in pounds and pence?

- If I borrow this money should I spend it or invest it?

- How does the loan get repaid?

Before you decide to release equity from your home you should talk to family members, a trusted friend or solicitor – if only to benefit from another person's view on the step you're taking. Once these arrangements are entered into, they are very difficult to reverse.

## I'm in my 60s – how much can I borrow?

This is one of the most commonly asked questions about equity release and the answer usually surprises people. There are very tight restrictions on the amount of your property's value that you can borrow and they are linked to your age. The younger you are, the smaller the proportion of your property's value that you will be able to borrow.

The lender – which is usually a bank, building society or insurance firm – will in almost all, if not all, cases provide a promise that the size of your loan will never exceed the value of your home. This is called the *no negative equity guarantee*. While such promises are the norm, it is still wise in every case to check the contract terms to ensure the promise is there in black and white.

This no negative equity guarantee means the lender is carrying quite a lot of risk. There is the risk that you will live for a very long time, which would push up the overall size of your loan (see below regarding the cost of the debt). There is also the risk that house prices might fall. As a result, lenders are cautious.

Table 10.1 comes from one major provider and highlights, by age, what proportion of your property you're allowed to borrow. It also shows that lenders charge bigger, riskier borrowers more. The more you want to borrow, the higher the rate of interest you'll have to pay.

**Table 10.1: How much of your home's value can you borrow?**

| Your age | Lowest interest rate (3.9%) | Moderate interest rate (4.3%) | Higher interest rate (5.6%) |
|---|---|---|---|
| 55 | 11% | 16% | 25% |
| 60 | 16% | 21% | 31% |
| 65 | 22% | 27% | 36% |
| 70 | 28% | 33% | 41% |
| 75 | 32% | 37% | 47% |
| 80 | 37% | 42% | 52% |
| 85 | 42% | 47% | 54% |

Where you are borrowing jointly with a spouse, the younger person's age is used by the lender in determining the amount that can be borrowed.

## How much will this borrowing cost me, in pounds and pence?

The most common types of equity release mortgages are known as *lifetime mortgages.*

They charge a fixed rate for as long as the mortgage remains in force. That period is unknown: it is likely to be as long as you live, or as long as you live in your home before going into care.

You do not make monthly repayments as with a normal mortgage. Instead, the interest rolls up over the years. The interest is compounded – meaning interest is charged on the interest already owing – and so the total debt can mushroom, especially if you are paying a high rate.

The value of your house might go up in the meantime – or it might go down. Either way the proportion of your property's value that you borrow at the outset is unlikely to remain the same throughout.

You might borrow one-third of your home's value, for example, at a high rate of interest (say 6%). After 30 years, assuming house price growth of less than 6%, your debts would be roughly two-thirds the value of your property.

Table 10.2 spells out a number of scenarios. It starts by assuming your home is worth £300,000 and that you borrow £100,000 at rates of 4.3%, 5% or 6%.

You will see that the second column assumes annual house price growth of 4%. While no one knows what will happen to house prices in the future, this is a conservative figure for annual growth based on house price movements in recent decades.

**Table 10.2: How compounded debts can rack up fast**

| What happens as the years go by? | Your property value (4% inflation) | The size of your debt at 4.3% | The size of your debt at 5% | The size of your debt at 6% |
|---|---|---|---|---|
| At the start | £300,000 | £100,000 | £100,000 | £100,000 |
| after 5 years... | £366,298 | £123,938 | £128,335 | £134,885 |
| 10 | £447,249 | £153,607 | £164,700 | £181,939 |
| 15 | £546,090 | £190,379 | £211,370 | £245,409 |
| 20 | £666,774 | £235,953 | £271,264 | £331,020 |
| 25 | £814,129 | £292,436 | £348,129 | £446,496 |
| 30 | £994,049 | £362,441 | £446,774 | £602,257 |
| 35 | £1,213,730 | £449,205 | £573,371 | £812,355 |

As you can see in the table, when you are not paying off the interest each month – as with a standard mortgage – the effect is to grow the total sum owed very quickly. That's because you are being charged interest on interest.

The higher the interest rate and the longer the loan, the more severe the effect, as you can see in the bottom right hand corner of the table.

There are ways to reduce the costs of the loan. Increasingly, equity release mortgages come with flexible features that can save money. One feature is a *drawdown* facility. With this, the lender effectively agrees a maximum sum that you can borrow. But you don't have to take it all at once. You will only pay interest on what you borrow.

Say your home is worth £600,000. The lender agrees that you may borrow £250,000. Instead of taking it all at once, however, you take just £50,000 to begin with, as that is the sum immediately required. You are not paying interest on the entire agreed sum – as most remains to be drawn down if and when you need it in future.

Another feature is an ability to pay the interest as you go, rather than letting it accumulate and compound. This can be very useful in certain situations as it keeps down the overall cost of the debt. But for this to work, you will need to have sufficient income to meet the monthly interest payments.

When people are borrowing capital against their home to give to children, for example, it may be that the children could help meet the monthly interest bills out of their own wages. This then becomes a cost-effective way of transferring capital down a generation. It could also help mitigate an inheritance tax liability where, for instance, those with large pension pots and valuable properties choose to live off capital raised via equity release and retain their pension intact. Because pensions are treated more generously for inheritance tax than property assets, savings can arise (see Chapters Seven and Eight for more on inheritance tax).

## If I borrow this money, should I spend it or invest it?

Equity release lenders have conducted numerous studies into what people do with the money they borrow. Rather disturbingly, these reports suggest that many people leave the capital that they have drawn from their home sitting in a bank account. This is very poor use of your asset.

Not only are you paying a high rate of interest, compounded, for the privilege of having that capital to hand, but it is earning nothing itself with interest rates at record lows.

*The simple rule is not to borrow unless you have a clear need for the cash.*

If you anticipate a future need for more money, make use of a flexible equity release arrangement where you can draw cash piecemeal, as it's needed.

## How does the loan get repaid?

The money is repaid on your death, or sooner if you sell the property to go into care.

Where a couple are mortgaged jointly the loan will run on until the second person's death, or until they go into care.

In most cases you are not able to settle the loan for other reasons without paying a penalty. If, for instance, you inherited money, you would probably be unable to use it to pay off the mortgage.

## The question of care costs

Elderly couples coming to grips with retirement finances are going to need to think about the costs of care.

Under current rules, people whose assets (including savings, investments and their home) exceed £23,250 in value are generally expected to pay all their care home fees. The thresholds in Wales and Scotland are higher at £30,000 and £26,500 respectively.

The vast majority of homeowners who release equity will still retain ownership of enough of their property to have to pay for care.

Indeed, local authorities have the power to pursue people who they believe might have disposed of assets deliberately in order to qualify for care assistance.

Either way, the issue of paying for care should be discussed by borrowers with their financial adviser (see Chapter Eleven) and, ideally, other family members, before signing up to an equity release arrangement.

## Homes are now the main storage tank of wealth for large swathes of Middle Britain

**Stephen Lowe** is a director of Just, an insurer that specialises in retirement planning and financing. He is an expert in care funding, equity release and specialised annuities.

\* \* \*

For a nation supposedly obsessed with property we have been reluctant to factor in the wealth tied up in our own homes when making financial plans for the future. That is now changing, driven in part by rising property values but also by a backdrop of lower returns and rising later life costs.

The over-55s have an estimated £1.8 trillion tied up in their homes in England alone, a figure forecast to double in the next two decades. Homes are now the main storage tank of wealth for large swathes of Middle Britain, perhaps not surprisingly given that many of us have poured more into mortgages than into our pensions.

Of course, homes are more than just financial assets. We live in our homes and have an emotional attachment to them through our families and the local community.

The most common type of equity release plan is the lifetime mortgage, and competition in the market has driven interest rates down and encouraged innovation. The majority of lifetime mortgages are at a fixed interest rate, with about two-thirds of users drawing down funds over time and the rest taking lump sums.

Strict consumer safeguards now apply to the equity release market, in terms of regulation and codes of practice. The Equity Release Council is a good source of advice and its members must adhere to a comprehensive set of rules, ensuring customers receive regulated advice from a qualified professional and use an independent solicitor.

Equity release is not well understood. Research by the Tax Incentivised Savings Association found that while two-thirds of people claimed to understand equity release, on average they could only answer three out of 13 true or false questions about it correctly. For example, nearly one-third incorrectly believed taking an equity release loan meant giving up legal ownership of the house.

While not suitable for everyone, it is worth exploring as a way to a more comfortable life. Equity release is certainly a solution worth investigating for anyone struggling for regular income or to pay off an interest-only mortgage, or who wants to release a lump sum to use or give away while they are still alive.

# Chapter Eleven
## Professional Advice

**"When will I need professional advice, where will I get it – and how much will it cost?"**

Anyone who's read this book thus far should have the confidence and knowledge to arrange their pension money successfully on their own. But that doesn't mean you won't sometimes need professional advice along the way.

This chapter outlines the key points before and during retirement when that advice is most likely to be necessary. It explains how to find an adviser and how much you should expect to pay for the advice.

If and when you do sit down with an adviser, keep this book to hand: it will help you ask the right questions and ensure you have a better understanding of any recommendations.

## When professional help is likely to be required

### Final salary company pension transfers and other guarantees

For those in their 50s, teeing up your pensions ahead of a planned retirement will be more or less complicated depending mainly on what workplace pension arrangements you have in place.

As covered in Chapter Two, if you have final salary (or defined benefit) pension entitlements, they are generally best left where they are. They will pay a guaranteed income underwritten by your former employer.

But if you need or wish – for whatever reason – to move these entitlements in the form of a cash lump sum into another pension, you'll need advice.

In fact it is a legal requirement – which will be made clear to you by the administrators of your company pension scheme – that you take financial advice if you wish to transfer benefits worth more than a certain value (currently £30,000).

This type of transaction is generally regarded as risky by financial advisers and many won't undertake it. They fear that they will be open to future complaints or litigation.

If you want to make such a transfer you need to tell your financial adviser upfront, to check whether they are prepared to take on your business. Such transactions can also be extremely expensive, with advisers wanting to take a percentage slice of the assets as their fee (see 'How much to pay', below).

Likewise, if you have pensions to which special benefits apply – such as guaranteed annuity rates – you might well need professional help to evaluate the worth of those guarantees before deciding to move or encash the pension.

## Tax and estate planning

Where you have substantial pension assets and/or a valuable property, you are probably going to need professional help at some point in order to avoid unnecessary tax.

The following four circumstances don't form a comprehensive list, but they are the most common triggers requiring people to seek tax advice in later life:

1. *Pension assets worth £1m or approaching £1m.* As covered in Chapter Seven, the current lifetime allowance – the maximum

you can save within a pension in a lifetime – is set at just over £1m. You can negotiate your way through this on your own, but the rules are still relatively new. You may need the reassurance of a tax professional's advice.

2. *Total assets including your property of more than £1m per married couple.* If you're in this position, inheritance tax is likely to be due on your estate following your death(s). There are some uncomplicated – and wholly legitimate – steps you can take to reduce this liability. Taking tax advice early on will give you opportunities to limit the bill.

3. *Marriage, divorce, death or inheritance.* As in all stages of life, these key events usually require a rearrangement of your financial affairs. If you're older there can be an element of urgency, as there is likely to be less time in which to manage tax liabilities or ensure that your wealth – pensions and everything else – is directed towards your chosen recipients.

4. *Drawing a large, one-off sum from your pension.* Remember that pension withdrawals are taxed as income (see Chapter Seven). If you need to make significant withdrawals, for example to help a child buy a property, you may need to plan this in order to avoid paying higher rates of income tax. Depending on the size and complexity of your other income, you might benefit from professional help.

## Equity release

The decision to mortgage your home in later life is so serious that there are specialist financial advisers who provide help with this alone. This is an advantage in some ways: you could expect a good equity release adviser to know all of the current available rates and options, for example, which is crucial for those who want flexibility in how they borrow (see Chapter Ten). But these advisers may not be as well qualified to see how your equity release arrangement will fit with your wider financial and tax circumstances.

# Where to find an adviser

If a friend or family member whose circumstances are similar to your own can recommend their financial adviser, start there. It's hard to beat a personal recommendation from someone you trust.

If you're not in this position, there are several useful directories published by advisers' trade bodies or other organisations.

These include:

## Unbiased.co.uk

An independent directory of professionals searchable by area and specialism.

## Vouchedfor.co.uk

An independent directory of advisers, also searchable by area and specialism, but with the difference that advisers are reviewed by clients.

## The Personal Finance Society

Part of the Chartered Insurance Institute, this is the professional body representing financial planners. It publishes a directory of advisers and chartered planners at www.thepfs.org/yourmoney.

## Moneyadviceservice.org.uk

This is the government's general financial information service. It includes a directory of financial advisers.

## Pensionwise.gov.uk

Another useful service set up by the government. It also offers a free phone-based or face-to-face appointment with a pensions specialist who can outline in broad terms your pension choices. It's not tailored advice. To qualify you need to be over 50 and *not* have any final salary pension entitlements. You can book your session online or by phone on 0800 138 3944.

## What sort of arrangement to strike with your adviser

Advice businesses fall broadly into two camps. There are those that will help with certain one-off situations as outlined above. And there are others that will want a longer-term relationship with you where, most likely, they oversee your investments for a percentage fee.

If you are comfortable managing your own investments – along the lines set out in the earlier chapters of this book – you shouldn't need the latter service. In this case, you are most likely to want help in relation to a specific need.

Bear in mind that even if you know what you want to achieve from seeing the adviser, he or she is going to want to go through a process which will probably require you to provide information about your wider circumstances. This is normal practice. Even in relation to a specific transaction, you should expect the adviser to follow roughly these steps:

- Conduct a *fact find*.
- Research options.
- Report to you with recommendations.
- Implementation.

In some cases, you might be able to do the implementation element on your own.

*What does execution-only mean?*

At various stages in the process of finding and dealing with an adviser, you may come across the term *execution only*. This is the technical description of a process where you are *not* being given advice. It is the opposite of full advice. You may encounter execution only, for instance, when you are buying an annuity.

At all times, ensure that you know whether or not you are receiving full advice and how much you are paying for it. All advisers should be very comfortable discussing fees and processes, and neither you nor they should feel embarrassed to talk at length about costs.

# How much to pay

If you require help with a particular scenario or situation, you're likely to pay either by the hour or a fixed fee for the work to be undertaken.

## By the hour

Depending on your location and the work, expect to pay anything up to £300 per hour. The average is around £150.

There are two dangers in paying by the hour. One is that you don't know at the outset what the full cost will be. The other is that you may feel deterred from asking questions. It's vital that you understand the advice and the recommended course of action and so, however you choose to pay, you should ask questions where necessary.

## A fixed fee per project

This may be more satisfactory in that you know from the start the costs involved. But you might be surprised at how high the costs can be. Here are some examples:

### Fixed fees for a range of scenarios

- Specialist advice on a defined benefit (final salary) pension transfer: £1,500.

- Advice on transferring a £100,000 pension with guaranteed annuity rates: £2,000.

- Converting a £100,000 pension pot into a lump sum and an annuity: £1,750.

- At-retirement advice where the client has a £200,000 pension, some final salary pension income, £100,000 of other savings and a £250,000 investment property, incorporating estate planning: £5,000.

Source: Unbiased.co.uk

---

## A fixed fee is the best way to pay for financial advice

**Billy Burrows** is one of Britain's best-known authorities on annuities and income planning in retirement. He has founded and worked for a number of firms specialising in annuities and is currently a director of the Better Retirement Group.

\* \* \*

One of the most frequently asked questions, apart from "How much cash can I get?" is "How much will it cost to get financial advice?"

The simple answer is that most advisers calculate fees as a percentage of the value of pension pots or funds they are working on. Or they charge a fixed fee.

Few advisers charge fees on an hourly basis unless for very wealthy clients with complex affairs.

I prefer a fixed fee for three reasons. First, it's easier to work out a fee that is fair to the client and economic for my business. Secondly, I think it is more professional because a percentage fee may not reflect the amount of work done, especially for larger pension pots. Thirdly, people know where they stand and know they can ask as many questions as they want without incurring extra charges.

One of the problems is that clients don't have a yardstick and don't know what value for money looks like. They may know the cost of a new car or kitchen, but have no idea what a fair price for advice is.

In my experience, the best way to deal with questions and concerns about fees is to take it step by step.

All elements of the service are explained and so are the methods of paying. If the client wants to pay via a deduction from their pension pot, that can be arranged. Or they can make a personal payment.

I explain that financial advice is good value for the following reasons. The stakes are high. Making the wrong decision could result in financial hardship or losing out financially. Some decisions relating to pension savings are likely to be the most difficult financial dilemmas you are likely to face in a lifetime. Getting help may be a wise investment. Finally, if advice is taken and things go wrong, the financial adviser will help put things right.

# Glossary

**Annuity**: an insurance contract under which an individual hands a lump sum to an insurer and in return the insurer pays an annual income until the policyholder's death. Extras such as annual increases and "spouses' benefits" – a stipulation that the policyholder's widow or widower will receive a payment after the policyholder's death – are available, although they reduce the annual income received for a given amount spent. Anyone whose medical condition or lifestyle choices (such as smoking) can be expected to reduce life expectancy should seek an "enhanced" or "impaired life" annuity, which will pay more each year to reflect the policy's likely shorter life.

**Annual allowance**: the maximum amount that can be paid into an individual's pension(s) each year and still qualify for tax relief. The allowance is £40,000 in the 2018–19 tax year, although anyone whose annual income exceeds £150,000 loses £1 of the annual allowance for each £2 of extra income, down to a minimum of £10,000. The allowance encompasses all contributions, including those made by employers and the notional amount deemed to be involved in any accrual of final salary benefits over the course of the year.

**Contracted out**: a pension saver was contracted out of top-up state pensions such as SERPS if they paid reduced National Insurance contributions on the basis that the money was instead paid into a workplace pension plan. Contracting out has now been abolished but some people who were contracted out at some stage of their career can expect a smaller state pension as a result of their reduced NI contributions.

**Coupon**: another word for the interest paid by a bond investment.

**Defined benefit pensions** (see final salary pension)

**Dividend**: the income paid by a share. Dividends can be paid annually, six-monthly, quarterly or monthly. Investment trusts and funds also pay dividends.

**Drawdown**: the term for the type of pension income on which this book is based – in other words, the withdrawal of dividends, coupons or the proceeds of asset sales from a pot of assets that remains invested after the saver has retired. The alternative to using drawdown is buying an annuity with the money that has accumulated in a pot of pension savings over the course of a worker's career.

**Equity income**: a name given to funds that generate income by investing in shares that pay dividends, as opposed to other assets such as bonds or property.

**Equity release**: a means of raising money in old age by borrowing against your home. Often there is no interest to pay while the borrower is alive. Instead, the interest is added to the loan and the entire sum repaid when the property is sold, either at death or when the borrower moves into a care home.

**Execution-only**: a description of financial transactions where companies simply do what you ask them to do as opposed to offering you advice. An execution-only stockbroker simply takes your instructions on which share to buy or sell and executes the trade on your behalf. When you use the investment platforms referred to in this book you are doing so on an "execution-only" basis.

**Final salary pension**: a pension, offered by your employer, that pays you a proportion of your salary when you retire. These pensions contrast with the type that form the basis of this book, where the saver builds up a pot of money in his or her own name, sometimes with the help of contributions from employers, and that money is used to generate income in retirement. With a final salary pension your employer is obliged to pay you, until you die, a set sum each month, calculated by reference to your final salary (or sometimes your career average salary). Because of the guaranteed payments, and mandatory inflation-linked increases, these pensions are seen as highly valuable.

**Fixed protection** (see lifetime allowance)

**Funds:** a collection of assets such as shares held by an investment management firm on behalf of individual or institutional investors, who own a set fraction of the fund in proportion to the amount they invested. Funds offer the advantages of diversification, which limits the damage caused if individual investments go wrong, and professional management. The fund management firm charges an annual fee of a percentage of the amount invested.

**Guaranteed annuity rate:** a special feature of certain savings plans taken out in previous decades. If you agreed to save into a pension with certain companies until you retired, you would be allowed to receive a predetermined sum from an annuity taken out with the same company. Without the guarantee you would have to accept whatever rate was offered in the market at the time, which, given how annuity rates have collapsed in recent years, would inevitably be much lower. Guaranteed annuity rates therefore tend to be extremely valuable and policyholders with such a rate should think very carefully before moving the money to another pension, which would see them forfeit the guarantee.

**Individual protection** (see lifetime allowance)

**ISA:** a savings plan with tax advantages. Up to £20,000 can be put into ISAs each year and invested in cash, stocks and shares and certain other assets. There is no tax rebate on money paid into an ISA, unlike with pensions, but investment growth and withdrawals are tax-free (although inheritance tax is payable on inherited ISAs).

**Lifetime allowance:** the maximum value that a pension pot (or series of pots held by the same individual) can reach before tax penalties apply. In the 2019–20 tax year the allowance is £1.055m. A saver's pension pots are assessed for compliance with the limit only at certain points: when the first money is withdrawn (whether as the tax-free lump sum, as the first income payment, perhaps from an annuity, or as an ad hoc withdrawal); at the age of 75; or if the pension is transferred overseas. Final salary pensions are included in the calculation of your total pension savings, using a notional value that multiplies your initial annual pension by a fixed figure. In some circumstances you can benefit from a higher allowance by using concessions called "fixed protection" and "individual protection".

**Market value adjustment**: a kind of exit penalty that can apply to with-profits investment plans if you want to take your money out early, perhaps because you want to transfer it to a self-managed pension.

**Natural yield**: the income generated by an asset such as a share, bond or property. The term is used to distinguish such income from money raised by the sale of a portion of such assets. For example, if your pension fund is invested in shares you can withdraw money either by taking just the dividends (the "natural yield") or by selling some of the shares, which some investors do on the basis that they expect the share price, in general, to rise.

**Passive funds** (see tracker funds)

**Pension pot**: a sum of money saved specifically in a pension as opposed to an ISA or other type of plan. A pension pot normally accumulates gradually over the course of a saver's working life, thanks to contributions from the saver (and perhaps from his or her employer) and to investment growth. On retirement the pension pot is normally used to generate income, either via regular withdrawals from the pot or via the use of the pot to buy an annuity. Final salary pensions do not involve a pension pot; here the worker simply accrues the right to a certain retirement income from his employer.

**Personal savings allowance**: a tax perk that allows interest from non-ISA savings accounts to be received tax-free. The allowance is £1,000 a year for basic-rate taxpayers (£500 for high-rate taxpayers) in 2018–19.

**Platform**: an online service that allows people to hold a wide variety of investments such as shares and funds in one place and switch easily between them. Those who follow the suggestions in this book will need to use a platform. The best known platforms include Hargreaves

Lansdown, Barclays Smart Investor, Fidelity Personal Investing and Interactive Investor.

**Tax code**: a combination of letters and numbers, issued by HMRC, that tells employers or pension companies how much tax to deduct from payments to employees or pension customers. All taxpayers should check periodically that their tax code is correct. Once you are past state pension age your tax code is likely to change to reflect the fact that you are receiving the state pension, which counts towards taxable income, without any tax deduction. There is therefore less additional income you can receive before you reach the personal allowance than there was before you became entitled to the state pension.

**Tax-free lump sum**: a benefit of saving in a pension by which 25% of a pension pot can be withdrawn free from income tax. Any withdrawals from the remainder of the pot are subject to tax in just the way that income from a salary would be.

**Tax relief**: the principal tax benefit of pensions. Pension contributions can be made from gross income, before tax is deducted. In practice this often means that savers pay into a pension from their taxed earnings and are then repaid the tax, either when their pension company claims a rebate on their behalf (and adds it to their pension pot) or when the taxpayer fills in a self-assessment return.

**Tracker funds**: a type of investment fund that does not attempt to "pick winners" but simply buys the shares or other assets that constitute a particular index, such as the FTSE 100. Tracker funds, also called passive funds, are becoming increasingly popular, partly because of scepticism on the part of some investors that professional fund managers can produce better returns than a tracker and partly because of these funds' low costs.

**Transfer value**: the sum offered to a member of a final salary pension scheme who wishes to cash it in for a lump sum, which would then be transferred to a "pension pot" style plan. Currently some transfer values are seen as very generous – perhaps 40 times the promised annual pension – and so many savers are accepting them. This involves taking on the risk and responsibility of investing the lump sum with the aim of producing a better income than the final salary scheme promised.

**Triple lock**: a promise from the government to increase the state pension in line with the higher of price or wage inflation, subject to a minimum of 2.5% a year. The triple lock is seen as generous but expensive and there have been consistent fears that it could be watered down in future.

**UFPLS (uncrystallised funds pension lump sum)**: a new means of withdrawing money from a pension pot, introduced as part of the pension freedoms. It involves dividing the pot into a potentially large number of "mini-pots" and treating each as a separate pension from which a 25% tax-free lump sum can be taken, as opposed to all in one go. Each mini-pot is "uncrystallised" (untouched) until its tax-free 25% cash is withdrawn. In some circumstances UFPLS can be more tax-efficient than taking one big tax-free lump sum and paying tax on all withdrawals thereafter.

**With-profits**: a type of investment fund that attempts to smooth out the ups and down of financial markets by holding back some gains in good years to hold in reserve for bad periods. All investors' money is pooled and an individual saver does not know how much they will get back until the plan matures. If they want their money back before maturity they may have to pay a penalty (see "market value adjustment"). With-profits investments, which started to lose favour about 20 years ago, are often held inside a pension.

**Yield**: the income that a share, bond or other investment produces as a proportion of its price. If a share is priced at £1 and pays an annual dividend of 4p, the yield is 4%.

# Index

173